# Critical Learning
# for Social Work
# Students

## Second Edition

## SUE JONES

Series Editors: Jonathan Parker and Greta Bradley

 |

Los Angeles | London | New Delhi
Singapore | Washington DC

Learning Matters
An imprint of SAGE Publications Ltd
1 Oliver's Yard
55 City Road
London EC1Y 1SP

SAGE Publications Inc.
2455 Teller Road
Thousand Oaks, California 91320

SAGE Publications India Pvt Ltd
B 1/I 1 Mohan Cooperative Industrial Area
Mathura Road
New Delhi 110 044

SAGE Publications Asia-Pacific Pte Ltd
3 Church Street
#10–04 Samsung Hub
Singapore 049483

Editor: Luke Block
Production controller: Chris Marke
Marketing manager: Tamara Navaratnam
Cover design: Wendy Scott
Typeset by: C&M Digitals (P) Ltd, Chennai, India
Printed in Great Britain by MPG Printgroup, UK

© Sue Jones 2013

First edition published in 2009 by Learning
Matters Ltd

Second edition published in 2013 by SAGE/
Learning Matters

Library of Congress Control Number: 2013934045

British Library Cataloguing in Publication Data

A catalogue record for this book is available from
the British Library

ISBN 978-1-44626-816-2 (pbk)
ISBN 978-1-44626-815-5

# Critical Learning for Social Work Students

# Contents

# Acknowledgements

My sincere thanks to Bachelor and Masters of Arts students at Manchester Metropolitan University who are currently undertaking their social work education, and to those who have done so over the past 23 years. You have stimulated my approach to critical aspects of learning about social work and prompted the writing of this book.

To colleagues in various learning and teaching fields from whom critical debate has both urged me onward and caused me to stop and reflect. Also to Luke Block and Helen Fairlie, from Learning Matters, whose support has been exemplary.

Not least to my family: Hollin for your technical expertise; Carrick for your thoughtful conversations; and to David for initial proof-reading and rapidly developing culinary expertise.

# Introduction to the second edition

Welcome to the second edition of *Critical Learning for Social Work Students*. During the past four years the publishers have received many useful reviews of the first edition from lecturers and practice educators; and as the author I have received much useful feedback from students. In the main these reviews indicated that the contents were very positively received. Some readers dipped into the book, using the exercises, while others asked their students to complete the log. Many commented on the usefulness of Chapters 2 and 3 where students needed to improve their study skills, while others focused on Chapters 1, 4 and 5 as crucial to the social work task. The range of readers came from across the academic field at both undergraduate and postgraduate levels, and from outside the social work discipline across healthcare allied professions. Some social work training sections were using the book on their staff development days and in supervision with qualified social work staff. Many of the most important elements for me as the author were the comments from students after using the book. They found that their academic grades had increased and their ability to participate in critical debate with confidence had risen considerably. In my role as assessor of students' work at undergraduate and Masters levels I could see the deepening of critical argument, informed questioning and ability to deal with both the nuances and the shifting nature of contemporary social work following their engagement with the book materials. I hope you find this edition equally stimulating, exercising, useful and at times fun!

## What's new in this edition?

There has recently been an imperative to lift social work higher into the professional domain. This has come from government, the profession and to some extent from service users and their carers who have experienced stigma in using services (Social Work Task Force (est. 2009), Social Work Reform Board (est. 2010)).

The first change you will notice is that the regulation of social workers and the standards they must meet has changed from the General Social Care Council (GSCC) to the newly renamed Health and Care Professions Council (HCPC). As a consequence, the National Occupational Standards, against which each chapter was referenced in the first edition, have been replaced with the Professional Capabilities Framework (PCF). (Please see below for a list of these new standards.) The ethical standards of the HCPC and the Standards of Practice for Social Work (SoPS) have replaced the previous Code of Conduct for Social Work Practice. The SoPS and PCF interrelate to provide clear statements of what is required of a social worker throughout the qualifying and post-qualifying period. Additionally, each Newly Qualified Social Worker (NQSW) must undergo a period of assessed post-qualifying practice. This is to be known as the Assessed Year in Employment (ASYE) and after successful completion of such an assessment, an NQSW may register with the HCPC in order to practise as a fully qualified social worker. The examples and activities in this edition will support you through your journey as a beginning student and into your ASYE.

Thirdly, I have included a new Chapter 5 about the skills needed to develop Emotional Intelligence (EI) and Appreciative Inquiry (AI), and I have threaded these ideas into some of the exercise examples presented in Chapter 5 to give you an idea of how you might further bring your 'use of self' into social work. EI and AI are two areas of learning that complement theory, received knowledge, experience and practice to recognise an appreciation of the individuals we are and the attributes we can bring to the human endeavour that is social work. Their constituents are surprisingly applicable and map easily over to the professional capabilities. Further, they bolster practitioners' professional armour in a climate of austerity where we can no longer expect monetary solutions to entrenched problems but simply look for smarter ways of working. Consequently, the previous Chapter 5 now becomes Chapter 6, with some revisions to reflect the use of EI and AI.

Additions to the worked examples have been influenced by the Munro Report (2011) on the prevention of child abuse and by the College of Social Work and their remit to rigorously represent social work in a professional manner to the media and the general public.

The new Professional Capabilities Framework for Social Workers in England contains nine domains:

- **Professionalism**

Identify and behave as a professional social worker committed to professional development.

- **Values and ethics**

Apply social work ethical principles and values to guide professional practice.

- **Diversity**

Recognise diversity and apply anti-discriminatory and anti-oppressive principles in practice.

- **Rights, justice and economic wellbeing**

Advance human rights and promote social justice and economic wellbeing.

- **Knowledge**

Apply knowledge of social sciences, law and social work practice theory.

- **Critical reflection and analysis**

Apply critical reflection and analysis to inform and provide a rationale for professional decision-making.

- **Intervention and skills**

Use judgement and authority to intervene with individuals, families and communities to promote independence, provide support and prevent harm, neglect and abuse.

- **Contexts and organisations**

Engage with, inform and adapt to changing contexts that shape practice. Operate effectively within your own organisational frameworks and contribute to the development of services and organisations. Operate effectively within multiagency and interprofessional settings.

- **Professional leadership**

Take responsibility for the professional learning and development of others through supervision, mentoring, assessing, research, teaching, leadership and management.

References to this Framework will be made throughout the text. You will find a diagram of the Professional Capability Framework in Appendix 1, on page 138, and relevant extracts from the Social Work Subject Benchmark Statement are in Appendix 2, on page 139.

Additionally, 10 of the 13 Standards contained within the HCPC Guidance on Conduct and Ethics for Students (GC&ES) are relevant to Social Work. These are:

1. You should always act in the best interests of your service users.

2. You should respect the confidentiality of your service users.

3. You should keep high standards of personal conduct.

6. You should keep your professional knowledge and skills up to date.

7. You should act within the limits of your knowledge and skills.

8. You should communicate effectively with service users and your education provider and placement providers.

9. You should get informed consent to provide care or services (so far as possible).

10. You should keep accurate records on service users.

12. You should behave honestly.

13. You should make sure that your behaviour does not damage public confidence in your profession.

Elements of the PCF and the GC&ES should interrelate to provide rigorous and critical evidence within your practice and portfolio of evidence.

In these exciting times, when we are on the verge of a deepening of professionalism within social work, new structures in practice and an emerging creativity through austerity, I trust this new edition will help you to fulfil your course requirements and yet more, to equip you with the skills and attributes that will launch you into your future careers.

# What is this book for?

The purpose of this book is to guide you through the attributes, skills, dispositions and abilities of critical learning to enable you to question, read, write and reason at deeper levels of understanding. This means showing you how you need to develop by using strategies and methods associated with critical learning at Year One, throughout your course and beyond.

The formative exercises and examples in the book will lead you towards developing these abilities and you will begin to see how elements of the 'critical' can be integrated into your work. This will reflect on the grades you can achieve as well as how you can begin to think about your practice differently. Some of this will be about how you know which words and phrases to use to express your ideas more professionally, but also that by using 'academic' language your thinking skills will move on more quickly and you will notice that you begin to integrate both deeper and broader views to inform your knowledge.

Through social work-related activities you will understand the academic qualities required in being a critical learner and be able to defend your views in such a way as to target more appropriately what markers are looking for in your work. Additionally, the skills of critical reasoning as a critical practitioner will enable you to demonstrate both your personal integrity and ability to bear the emotional content of the work, and to hold a knowledgeable position within an anti-oppressive and anti-discriminatory framework. All this recognises social work as a contested activity, subject to change and having views about social policy and the law, local, national and international communities and cultures, influential stakeholders and the sense of yourself within the work. Of course, critical skills used in social work are also common across other professions, in health and education, and so some examples reflect the integrated nature of a multiprofessional workforce.

# What is 'critical'?

In professional life, and especially where working directly with others, users of social care services, their carers, colleagues and other professionals, you will be developing a sensitivity to appreciate positions of which you have no experience.

You will need to be careful that you don't:

- unintentionally misuse your power;
- misunderstand key issues of discrimination and oppression;
- fail to recognise significant events;
- minimise the need to take action.

And that you do:

- step back and reflect on your practice and that of others;
- recognise the potential for discrimination and oppression;
- consider a wide range of influential factors;
- take informed action where there is actual or potential risk.

In learning how to do these last four you will be developing the following abilities.

- **Critique** See the nuances as well as the obvious in what you read and hear. This is not like 'criticism' where there is a tendency to see only the negative aspects. A critique would offer a balanced view of all aspects.

- **Analyse** Be discerning about how you gather information and recognise the significance of its structure and constituent parts. This means not only choosing those aspects of an issue that agree with what you think but also those that are counter to your beliefs.

- **Evaluate** Judge the quality and importance or value of something. This is about how you are able to weigh up what significance something would have to your argument.

- **Synthesise** Fuse different ideas together to create a new 'whole'. This is how you are able to make connections between ideas with the result that you create new perspectives, usually those with more complexity than previously imagined. It involves deductive reasoning, and often the resolution of conflict created by opposing positions or arguments.

- **Reframe** Create a new position for an argument. This is how you see that critical learning has taken place because you are able to let go of previously-held views by replacing them with your new understandings.

You will also learn to deal with the following challenges.

- **Dilemmas and tensions** The deep thinking needed for critical engagement will cause you to continue to question yourself even when the answer appears to be easy. You will become aware that surface level thinking leads to inadequate understanding and creates simplistic solutions.

- **Unknowing** The realisation that in any area you cannot have all the information or know the absolute truth. Usually you will be working with nuances, alternative perspectives to your own, and any decisions you make can only be tentative, 'good enough' in the moment, and must be open to rethinking.

- **Uncertainty** In order to flourish, professionals need to be able to cope with self-doubt. You are a human being and we make mistakes. Use these occasions for growth, take from them learning experiences and recognise them as integral to the experience of working with the uniqueness of the human condition in an ever-changing environment.

- **Emotional confusion** Professional life is peppered with elation and despair. One day it is the best thing in the world, the next it can be the worst, and other days it can be anywhere in between from run of the mill to exhilarating. Learning how to deal with this roller coaster is fundamental to your own well-being and you will do well to draw around you a support network with which to share, commiserate and advise on your practice.

In summary, these nine areas form the constituent parts of the critical when attached to questioning, reading, writing, reasoning, thinking and to practice, analysis, evaluation and synthesis. Another way to understand what critical elements are is that they are those things that cause you to be restless and unsatisfied when you feel you have not fully explored or 'bottomed' all aspects of something. It is rather like having a small biting insect that keeps trying to bite you even though you keep wafting it away. Give the insect some thought and you might trap it in a box and put it outside, remove yourself from the room, put up a fly trap or spray yourself with fly repellent. When you next encounter such a fly you will know how to deal with it effectively! So it is with the critical fly; meet it head on and it will become increasingly easier and effective to use.

# Who are you?

Maybe you have lots of experience in social care work, perhaps you are coming into university straight from completing formal education or from doing a part-time access course, HND or NVQ programme. You may be a carer for your family or loved one(s), or have been until recently and now see this as your time to develop your career in social work. Whatever your route to social work education you will probably be apprehensive about what will be expected of you academically. For this reason I have created six chapters that I hope will nurture you through stages to become a more critical learner and ultimately a practitioner who is full of thought, able to respond to constantly shifting agendas in social care, possesses integrity and deep learning, and can bear the emotional content of the work you have elected to do.

# How will this book help me and how will I begin?

In order to begin the process you need to know how to pose questions for yourself and for others that will initiate the process of critical learning. In Chapter 1, 'Developing critical questions', I offer you a scaffold of four question types to help you with this activity. Next you will be building on your knowledge by undertaking the chapter 'Developing critical reading', and here you will find some strategies to help you to become a more strategic reader. The third chapter, 'Developing critical writing', shows you how to plan, evidence, create connections, use logical flow and be coherent. Chapter 4 demonstrates how you might be 'Developing critical reasoning' by using deductive and inductive arguments, logic and truth contesting to evidence your arguments. Chapter 5, 'Developing a critical approach using multiple intelligences', does exactly that. Using Emotional Intelligence (EI) and Appreciative Inquiry (AI) will enable you to recognise and develop a solution-focused approach to working with colleagues in agencies that drives forward action and change positively. The final chapter, 'Developing as a critical practitioner', brings all the previous attributes, skills and knowledge to bear on your practice in placement and in readiness as a qualified registered practitioner moving on to post-qualifying levels.

Throughout the book you will find exercises and activities. Some of these ask you to record your learning in a learning log. I have provided a sample template for you to use at the end of the book. Just photocopy and enlarge this as often as you need to. You might also give this as evidence of learning if your programme requires you to produce a portfolio of learning.

You should be reassured that most students feel apprehensive, even those who have previously completed degrees and are now joining the social work programmes at Master's level. In today's fast-moving learning environments, especially in social work where the curriculum is already very crowded, it would be wonderful to say that new technologies have provided us with a way to avoid reading. While many of our students are highly adept at using the web, accessing e-journals on the computer and using Wikipedia to root out information and where lecturers provide reading lists, book extracts, blogs and Web activities online, we need to remember that all these activities involve reading. There is no substitute for reading, yet a more critical approach can help you to develop strategic skills that will save you time.

# Chapter 1

## Developing critical questions

## Introduction

This first chapter will introduce you to some of the skills and strategies used in posing critical questions. You will work with a framework that will support you from the fundamental to the critical level of question-posing and provide you with a good bedrock from which to develop your ideas. Essentially a framework is usually provided to support something but it can be taken down once the skill level has been achieved. So it is with learning to ask critical questions: once you know how to do this you will find yourself doing it all the time without needing to work your way up the framework. Asking critical questions is vital to intellectual development because they push the boundaries of our knowledge. We may even ask questions for which we have no answers at the time. By asking them we consciously search for answers or nuances of statements that might be answers. What we experience is a 'process' activity, that is using intellectual strategies to attempt to reach an outcome – perhaps an answer. The importance is vested in the journey of discovery rather than in the discovery itself. It could be said that what might constitute 'answers' now would not do so in the future and in order to 'future-proof' social work our students need to develop critical thinking skills that lead to them asking the correct questions rather than seeing that there is necessarily one right answer. There are some fun activities and quizzes for you to do in this chapter too.

By the end of this chapter you will be able to:

- create questions that will lead you to be more critical in composing your assignments;
- reflect on how to move from fundamental question-posing to critical question-posing;
- judge your current critical questioning abilities;
- use your critical learning log to identify areas for further development.

# Four question types as a 'scaffold' to critical questioning

The first stage in critical learning is the ability to pose critical questions. It is easier to begin by thinking about where critical questions come from. The journey begins by starting with the basics; for example, these would be your fundamental ideas and moving through how these connect to each other and to other ideas. The next stage is to link these connecting ideas to create an hypothesis. This is about how the quality of your thinking moves on to consider broader and deeper implications, and how you can defend these based on what you now know. The final stage is to consider what is known but also what might not be known; the nuances or shades within your knowledge and the dilemmas this might create for you. In social work this stage would take in the social, cultural, political and economic agendas, causing us to view each situation from a multi-dimensional perspective. This is referred to as the critical stage because it demonstrates a critique of the expanse and rigour of learning.

(This four-stage questioning analysis has been developed from an idea at http://academic. cuesta.edu/acasupp/as/622.htm Counselling and Development Centre, 145 Behavioural Sciences Building, York University 4700 Keele St, Toronto, ON M3J 1P3.)

---

ACTIVITY **1.1**

*Look at the following table and see if you can position where you think you are at present. Begin your learning log by writing what stage you think you are at and why.*

*For example, what sort of comments are you receiving on your academic work? Set yourself a task to improve to the next level by writing out questions for each level for your next assignment question.*

---

*Table 1.1 Stages towards asking critical questions*

| Question type | Description | Attributes |
|---|---|---|
| Fundamental | What do I think/know about X? | describing, underpinning points with quotations |
| Connecting | How does X relate to Y and Z? | judging, balancing different perspectives, identifying a major contender in the debate |
| Hypothesis | If X relates to Y and Z then A | consolidation, creativity, positioning a new perspective |
| Critical | How can I defend my argument in evaluating X,Y Z and A? | contemplation, lateral thinking, conceptualisation of micro and macro debates and posing insightful explanations, solutions and/or challenges |

Here is an example that may help you.

---

ACTIVITY **1.2**

### Lone mothers

Q *Consider the position of lone mothers and whether they are supported or penalised by current government policy.*

**Fundamental questions** *you might ask yourself.*
*What is current government policy about lone mothers?*
*Why was it created?*
*Is it helpful to them or not?*

**Connecting questions** *you might ask yourself.*
*What societal ideas promoted the policy development?*
*Is the policy based on sound evidence?*
*What do lone mothers think about the helpfulness of the practice promoted by the policy?*

**Hypothesis questions** *you might ask yourself.*
*How could I assess the 'fit' between the policy and the practice from the government's and the lone mother's perspective?*
*What effect does the policy and practice have on other stakeholders, e.g. fathers, employers, schools, the economy, children's (perceived) potential?*
*How successful have the implementation and effect been for the government and lone mothers?*

**Critical questions** *you might ask yourself.*
*Can I propose a challenge, offer a potential solution, and raise further questions, for example about morality and the ethics of compulsion?*
*What theories might I use to offer an explanation of why I think this situation occurred?*
*How can I use these theories to underpin or lead my argument and also link this into a practice element that I could use on placement?*

# Comment

Here are some possible answers that might result from these different types of questioning. These are short examples only but they give you the gist of the type of responses that the questions promote.

### Fundamental answer
I know that government policy on lone mothers focuses on giving opportunities for work to lift them out of poverty.

### Connecting answer
I know that government policy promotes this view of lone mothers because they are blamed for raising delinquent youths due to having no male disciplinarian. The view is that these women perpetuate a circle of dependency by being claimants and by raising children who underachieve and then find it difficult to obtain work.

### Hypothesis answer
I also know that there is no evidence to suggest that delinquency resides with lone mother households. I have read that income maintenance for this group is inadequate. There is no access to affordable childcare, absent fathers fail to accept responsibility for their children, employers are inflexible, and part-time work is poorly paid and insecure. This leads to lone mothers being stigmatised by social policy and media promulgation of blame.

### Critical answer
In addressing the effect of government policy on lone mothers it is clear that the argument is strongly weighted towards a system that penalises vulnerable women [evidence this] who may already be earnestly seeking employment and those who, after considered thought, make a decision to remain unemployed while their children are young. Evidence suggests [give a reference here] that the social construction of 'motherhood' and of 'lone mothers' is increasingly creating a blame culture that fails to recognise the need for more appropriately targeted equality measures. These would include better community networks, advocacy and mediation services, sustainable support of income maintenance and challenging the role of women as being the only carers of children through a cabinet-level office of Minister for Women. These strategies would raise the profile of lone women carers as nurturers of the next generation and expose the current oppressive policy/practice. A newly created discourse on lone motherhood would make connections between feminist theories of the rights of women, the labelling from societal discourse about women as lone mothers, and the position of children and young people as our next parental generation. In this way the binary of middle-class male dominance would be challenged by an oppositional binary of working women and their rights to accessible and appropriate support as of right, and not because they are inadequate, weak and dependent members of society.

You will see that the answers to the fundamental and connecting questions are not wrong but they lack any depth. They can be said to be surface-level answers. They might be useful in an introduction or in setting the scene.

The hypothesis response begins to broaden out the answer to consider the position of others within the debate, and of how opinion-makers in powerful and influential positions perpetuate ideas about others who are in less powerful or oppressed positions. This is not to say that all lone mothers feel this but that the odds are stacked against them. This response would demonstrate that you are able to take a 'helicopter view' (DeBono, on www.mindtools.com) and broaden your understanding by questioning what you read, making evidenced links and applying your new knowledge to practice.

You would be contemplating what the actual and alternative responses might be to the question.

Finally, a critical answer would show how you had thought logically, deeply and reflectively about the issue, and were able to interpret the substance of the issues and pose insightful and challenging questions, create solutions, employ a persuasive use of theory, contemplate the micro and macro issues (subjective personal and objective public implications), and conceptualise how the existing 'discourse' (ways of thinking) about lone mothers could be replaced by one commensurate with anti-oppressive values.

---

### ACTIVITY **1.3**

*Consolidation quiz*

*This is a True/False quick quiz to help you to consolidate your learning so far. It is also a little light-hearted. Powell and Andresen (1985) have emphasised that humour is a great source of support while learning so hopefully you will spot such elements in my quiz.*

**Statement   Indicate whether you think this is true or false**                            **T/F**

1. *Fundamental questions are those that really get to the bottom of the issue.*
2. *An hypothesis question can only result from having done lots of very focused reading.*
3. *A connecting question means I would write about only two opposing views in the assignment.*
4. *Critical questions are those that deal with emergencies of some kind.*
5. *Fundamental questions don't stretch us to understand at deeper levels.*
6. *An hypothesis question is based only on my own views.*
7. *Asking connecting questions would help me to see alternative views.*
8. *Critical questions allow for deeper learning.*
9. *A connecting question would enable me to demonstrate how I used the telephone.*
10. *A fundamental question would help me in working with people who were experiencing mental ill health.*
11. *A critical question would provoke some challenge to me by posing a question that I couldn't currently answer.*
12. *A hypothesis question is one used only when completing a thesis.*

Before you look at the answers at the end of this chapter, read these helpful hints to check your answers.

In the case of types of questions a fundamental approach is seen to be basic. It provokes responses that are one-dimensional. It is the place we might start to research an issue so that by asking some simple (fundamental) questions such as what, when, who, how and sometimes why, we start to be aware of our subject. Having understood some elements of our answer it is easy to think we will have done all that is required, and it is tempting to go on to plump out the work with assumptions, long quotations and rhetoric. (This means making statements such as *Why do they allow this to happen?* and *I wonder if these politicians would be able to live on such low benefits?*) These strategies don't allow you to demonstrate your arguments well and they may even lose you marks for lack of clarity and focus.

In order to improve your questioning techniques, try asking the question 'whether'. This allows you to broaden your views and to take in more than one perspective that will then lead you into the 'connecting' questions level.

---

**ACTIVITY 1.4**

*Suppose your question is:*
  Why have lone mothers rejected government attempts to force them back to work? *(This is a fundamental question.)*

*You might develop this into:*
  What evidence is there that lone mothers have rejected government attempts to force them back to work? *(This makes you look at ideas that connect and moves you to think in a more critical way about the issue.)*

*Have a look at your next assignment question and see if you can identify what the fundamental, connecting, hypotheses and critical questions might be.*

---

## Comment

Think about the notion of connecting as being more like a human body than a hosepipe. The human body functions as much more than its constituent parts. It is permeable and impulses flow to and from and across its dimensions and extremities. Similarly, ideas, thoughts and consequently questions flow in between each other and stimulate new responses that are acted upon and create new perspectives. In contrast, a hosepipe connects two things together and then does not allow anything to escape or be imbibed that might 'contaminate' the environment until it reaches its conclusion. (Of course, we know that hosepipes leak and so it is that even when you ask a simplistic connecting question you are likely to engage in some level of judgement.)

One way to improve your connecting question technique is to ask what the impact might be upon the theme under debate. This will push you to examine the effect from different perspectives in an incremental way. You might begin with whether some lone mothers have always wanted to engage in work but societal structures and employer and media attitudes have created ideas about them that were stereotypical and negative. You might then go on to look at where these ideas come from and how they are woven into the fabric of society.

---

ACTIVITY **1.5**

*Therefore you might now think:*

How can lone mothers even begin to return to work when childcare is so expensive and being claimants they are dependent on low-income maintenance?

*So your question would be:*

What would the impact of being a benefit claimant have on lone mothers who are attempting to seek employment?

*You can see that this question links ideas together – lone motherhood, benefit claimant and employment – in a way that pushes you to examine the implication more than just stating what appears to be fact.*

*Can you begin to think through the next stage, hypothesis questions? How might you now move your questioning technique forward by developing this last question?*

---

## Comment

The word 'hypothesis' means:

*An idea which is thought suitable to explain the facts about something.*

(*Longman Dictionary of Contemporary English*, 1981)

also:

*A tentative explanation for a phenomenon, used as a basis for further investigation.*

(*Encarta*, 1999)

Looking back to the hypothesis text, you will see that several ideas were put forward resulting in the statement *lone mothers are stigmatised by social policy and media promulgation of blame*. This statement becomes the author's 'hypothesis'; something they have come to understand but that now needs further investigation. So in one respect it is the views of the author that are represented but it has to be shown that these views have been informed by relevant reading of authoritative texts, research, journals or websites.

The word 'thesis' may be known to you as a lengthy academic paper commonly presented as evidence of an ability to study at doctoral level (at undergraduate and Masters level the final such work is normally referred to as a 'dissertation'). However, it is also used to refer to:

*an opinion or statement put forward and supported by reasoned argument.*

(*Longman Dictionary of Contemporary English*, 1981)

You might say that in asking yourself hypothetical-type questions you are creating an informed argument in order to come to some preliminary position and understanding that will be open to revision after further investigation.

To improve your hypothesis questioning, link the development of your ideas with evidence of your research and how you might agree with or refute the propositions of others.

---

*ACTIVITY* **1.6**

*You could use this technique to present opposing views, act as a protagonist with your source(s) – this means offer evidence against their positions, and even expose your uncertainties where you are unconvinced by what you read.*
> How do my ideas link together to produce a proposition *[statement of opinion or judgement]* about lone motherhood?

*Or better:*
> In what way does the reading I have done consolidate my thinking and synthesise my arguments towards a revised position about lone mothers, delinquency and employment?'

*Try to write a hypothesis question for yourself. Use your next assignment question if it helps.*

---

## Comment

You will need to get used to using words like 'consolidate', 'refute', 'proposition', 'synthesis of ideas' and 'revised position'. Using this language signals to the reader that you are understanding the importance of academically expressing your ideas and arguments.

In everyday life the word 'critical' is more normally applied to some emergency situation or implies adverse comments being made in order to find fault. In academic life 'critical' means:

> *giving comments or judgements – containing or involving comments and opinions that analyse or judge something, especially in a detailed way.*
>
> *Associated meanings also include crucial, essential, undergoing change.*

(*Encarta,* 1999)

In asking yourself such questions you will undertake research and contemplate what the issues might be. To do this you will have built up an insight into the issues in the debate and be able to conceptualise what the agreements and challenges might be. They may not actually be so but if you are able to defend your position by good evidence and reasoning, then this will be reflected in your grade.

Some of the most interesting work is where students/academics have challenged taken-for-granted assumptions and offered alternative explanations and solutions. For example, social structures are mostly created by those in power who are usually white, middle-class males who generally are not aware of the implications for lone mothers living in poverty. It follows, then, that in a capitalist society those who create such structures do so under the influence of economic rationality. It is better to have people in work contributing to the tax system rather than taking money out as benefits. They may underpin their reasons with supplementary arguments such as the potential for the creation of an 'underclass' that is perpetuated through generations of lone motherhood, propensity for crime and disorder among young males and early pregnancy in girls from such households. So, a whole discourse (way of thinking) is created within a blame culture.

Alternatively, a student, understanding about such societal views, might articulate (defend a position), a view that stems from the views of lone mothers themselves. These positions might incorporate death of a parent in early life, disadvantage in schooling, peer expectations and limited employment opportunities, leading to poor self-image and a lack of social capital (social, cultural and educational advantages). The latter position would highlight the responsibility of opinion-makers in society to respond to these dilemmas by developing ways to bring equity to those in oppressed positions – like lone mothers. This signifies the level at which critical questions can stimulate insight while engaging with and challenging the social construction of public problems.

In asking yourself critical questions, ask what the implications might be in applying an alternative approach. You may have some 'favourite' theoretical friends, for example, Thompson, anti-discriminatory practice, and Oliver, social model of disability, that have served you well in the past. You could use these, but also you need to explore theories that are central to the theme – in this case feminist theories and those relating to the social construction of childhood, employment and educational opportunities.

---

### ACTIVITY 1.7

*Here is an example of a critical question you might ask yourself:*
   In what ways could theories about the different types of feminisms be used to refute the status quo (taken-for-granted assumptions) about lone mothers?

*Or better:*
   What would be the implications of applying alternative theoretical approaches to the current government policy on lone motherhood?

*It is the second example that would deepen your critical answers. The first example is not incorrect but would not generate such a deep response.*

*Using one of your assignment titles, go to your learning log now and write some critical questions for yourself.*

---

## Comment

You may find this difficult as you will be posing the question *Is that a critical question?* Try revisiting the True/False quiz and see if you are still so certain of your answers.

ACTIVITY *1.8*

Revisit the true/false quiz and analyse your previous answers. Are you quite so certain about them now?

## Comment

Don't worry – you should now be able to see that in most of the questions there are shades of truth. This is a good attitude to have when addressing your academic learning. It is the ability to bear the uncertainty of knowledge claims and a useful attribute when we come to the final chapter on 'Developing as a critical practitioner'.

# Critical questions – interpretations, shades and nuances

You might have realised that some of the examples were partly true and partly false. Questions 1, 2, 3, 4, 6, 10 and 12 contain nuances or shades of truth and falsehood. For example, Q1 states that:

*Fundamental questions are those that really get to the bottom of the issue.*

We all have to begin somewhere and the beginning of the journey to 'get to the bottom of an issue' might begin by asking a fundamental question.

Also, Q12 states that:

*An hypothesis question is one used only when completing a thesis.*

PhD students create an hypothesis that they set out to interrogate through their thesis. This is true but it doesn't mean that it is only at that level that ideas come together in the form of a 'thesis'. We might instead call it an 'argument' or a 'position' that is put forward in an assignment. Therefore the words 'thesis' and 'hypothesis' are applied to all forms of academic thinking and writing regardless of the level of study – PhDs included.

Some of the skills of choosing what sort of questions to ask and how to interpret the answers can be developed as attributes or dispositions. These can be described as follows.

*Clear thinking, logical, thoughtful, attentive to the facts, open to alternatives, use of knowledge and experiences to lead ideas, prepared to give up own agendas when faced with persuasive arguments, responsible for self-regulation, able to interpret thoughts and knowledge and to synthesise learning, ability to deduce, analyse, evaluate and explain simply the meaning and significance of events and knowledge at micro and macro levels, form reasoned judgements.*

By striving to develop the skills associated with these attributes and dispositions you will begin to realise that the essential quality of asking a range of questions is in being able to de-personalise and de-blame your questioning technique.

For example, have a look at these questions.

Q1 *Why are older people being forced to live in poverty?*

This indicates that you already have a view that confirms older people are living in poverty. You will base your arguments on that premise (statement) and will be disposed to search out texts and quotes that support your views.

Q2 *Do older people live in poverty?*

This is a more open question that will cause you to look for evidence to support that older people are or are not living in poverty.

Q3 *What are the alternatives for those older people living in poverty?*

This enables you to demonstrate that some older people may not be living in poverty but you are going to concentrate on those who are. This question would encourage you to think about public policy, perhaps some creative schemes like 'adopt a granny', supported housing, liberal education (a place to be with peers while stimulating the mind, having a meal and being warm), better support for carers, non-traditional families, other cultural practices and increased income maintenance.

Q4 *What are the causes and implications of older people living in poverty?*

In this question you would be bringing together the deeper debates related to the social construction of 'older age'. How have our ideas about older age been shaped through history, different cultures, globalisation, economic rationality (values those who are contributing into a capitalist system, for example, through payment of taxes but 'throws away' those who leach the system through drawing benefits, increased healthcare needs and dependency on public provision). You would be getting into some controversial debates such as euthanasia, demographic changes, restricting health provision for those who are judged to have caused their own ill health by their behaviour – the 'undeserving' – and the application of a medical model of support that sees people as a collection of symptoms and inabilities rather than as human beings. The revolving-door strategy of hospitals in prematurely releasing older patients back into the community in order to meet treatment targets is an example of this. The health authorities can charge social services departments if they fail to find community placements and this is evidence of tactics in blaming older people for 'bed-blocking'. This practice destroys the fledgling multi-professional collaboration required by the Health and Social Services Joint Planning Boards.

Perhaps you might place yourself in the position of an older person and be able to see that in comparison with regulated residential care, the option of retaining one's independence but living in poverty is one that many older people choose to take. It is often as a result of concern from family members, the medical profession or neighbours that you are asked to intervene as a social worker. Your remit will be to resist these external pressures and to support the older person in their wishes while balancing the various levels of risk that would apply. This question would allow you to debate issues of ageing, public and private problems, coercion, risk and the prevailing discourse (way of thinking) about older people by using research, theory, best-practice publications (see SCIE) and by situating

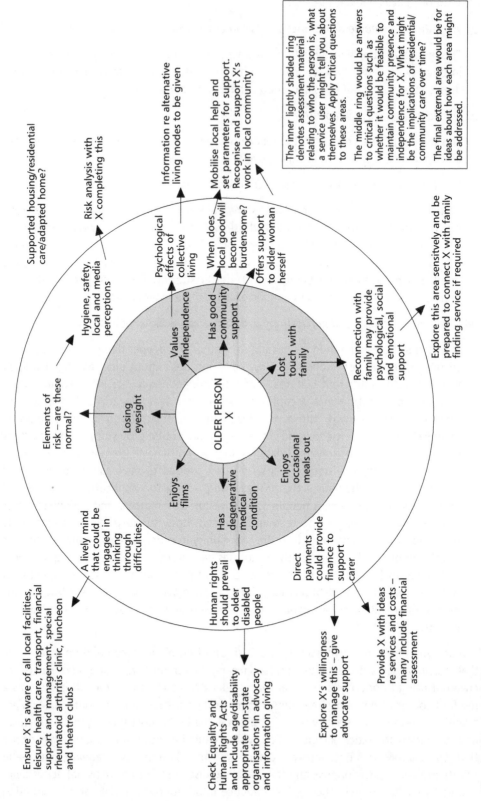

The inner lightly shaded ring denotes assessment material relating to who the person is, what a service user might tell you about themselves. Apply critical questions to these areas.

The middle ring would be answers to critical questions such as whether it would be feasible to maintain community presence and independence for X. What might be the implications of residential/community care over time?

The final external area would be for ideas about how each area might be addressed.

Supported housing/residential care/adapted home?

Risk analysis with X completing this

Information re alternative living modes to be given

Hygiene, safety, local and media perceptions

Psychological effects of collective living

When does local goodwill become burdensome?

Mobilise local help and set parameters for support. Recognise and support X's work in local community

Offers support to older woman herself

Elements of risk – are these normal?

Values independence

Has good community support

Lost touch with family

Reconnection with family may provide psychological, social and emotional support

Losing eyesight

OLDER PERSON X

Explore this area sensitvely and be prepared to connect X with family finding service if required

A lively mind that could be engaged in thinking through difficulties

Enjoys films

Has degenerative medical condition

Enjoys occasional meals out

Ensure X is aware of all local facilities, leisure, health care, transport, financial support and management, special rheumatoid arthritis clinic, luncheon and theatre clubs

Human rights should prevail to older disabled people

Direct payments could provide finance to support carer

Check Equality and Human Rights Acts and include age/disability appropriate non-state organisations in advocacy and information giving

Explore X's willingness to manage this – give advocate support

Provide X with ideas re services and costs – many include financial assessment

*Figure 1.1 Ripple diagram*

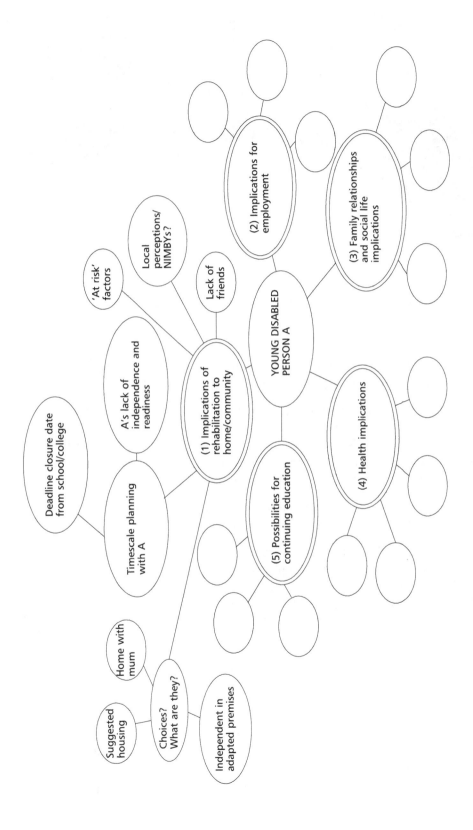

*Figure 1.2 Spider diagram. Five areas have been identified and each is capable of further dissection. Can you complete the whole spider diagram?*

*Figure 1.3 Using visual images for critical thinking*

yourself as a social worker within the debate. In this way you would be demonstrating how, in working with older people, all these debates will impact on you too.

In thinking about the sorts of questions to ask, you can see that in Q2 to Q4 you will need to do some research to inform how you think and the knowledge you have about older people other than the experiences and knowledge you might already have in that area. This personal knowledge is important and relevant but by just basing your ideas upon it you will be limiting the development of your 'critical' abilities.

Would you like to try posing some questions to help you with one of your assignments? Try to follow the example above – beginning at Q2 level.

Sometimes it helps to think about critical questions if we represent our thinking visually. Here are some ideas to help you. Ripple and spider diagrams – these help us to put our ideas together on one page in a way that gets away from linear thinking. So instead of thinking: older people – independent living – health – resourcing costs, etc., you can develop your ideas along the lines of Figures 1.1, 1.2 and 1.3.

Visual images create powerful snapshots of our lives or an event for us to reflect upon. The photograph in Figure 1.3 was taken at Christmas. The boy is now an adult and the grandparents have died. At the time the photograph was taken, relationships had been affected by generational differences and there was conflict about whether mothers should work, husbands push for promotion, children be given so much freedom. Our views about how much involvement grandparents should have with their grandchildren were influenced by our peers and friends, the experiences of our own childhoods and local proximity, or not. This thinking is now being revisited as we become the grandparents and the little boy in the photograph a parent himself. Using visual images is a highly effective way of working with service users who don't use words.

As an example you could take three ideas (these are adapted from 'Approaches to studying inventory' by Entwistle and Ramsden (1983) and further developed in a study by Heikkila and Lonka in Finland in 2006).

# Metaphor

A metaphor uses an idea to stand for something else. Here is an example of how we might use a kit bag as a metaphor for an older person.

> *I am a kit bag full of knowledge, history, experiences, memories, excitements and disappointments. I have pockets full of skills in solving problems, making the best and the most of things, knowing how to let go and how to welcome back children long gone. At the top I put the apprehensions, uncertainties, anxieties and fear that increasingly encroach into my life now. Right in the middle I find solace in the person I have become over the years, in my integrity and patience, and knowing I have had a life well lived.*

Using this technique and speaking as if you are that person leads to greater empathy, creative thinking and exposes your own values. For some, using the metaphor of a kit bag could lead to buying a powerful motorbike and hitting the road at an older age.

# Recording your learning – Keeping a learning log

After you have gone through an experience designed for your learning, it is useful to ask yourself some questions about it. You may not have found an experience useful and in some ways it is more meaningful if you use these experiences to analyse why they were not helpful and to indicate how you could adapt or replace them with something of more benefit. Your learning log should not be an outpouring of your feelings but a record of what worked, what didn't, the implications, why and how it could be improved.

# What sort of a learner am I?

It will come as no surprise to you that we all learn differently. Here are some descriptions and examples of types of learning and learner.

*Achievement learner* identify what is the best possible attitude you (could) have to learning.

> *It is important for me to do really well on the course.*

Example: *I didn't only study the books about Task Centred practice from the reading list but also followed up with my practice teacher about how this method could be used to incorporate empowerment and advocacy within the placement.*

*Deep learner* demonstrate an element of how you deepened your learning.

> *I usually set out to learn (understand) thoroughly ... what I am asked to read*

Example: *I felt unsure about the cognitive behaviourist theories and so I asked my practice teacher/tutor if we could go through the text and explore my understanding more critically.*

*Surface learner* draw out where you have done a task only superficially.

> *The best way for me to learn (understand) … is to memorise textbook definitions.*

Example: *I didn't fully understand what I read and so I used quotes in my work but really this was just to mask the fact that I didn't learn anything from what I read.*

We all use a mixture of these three and at its best this can be called Strategic Learning. However, if you really want to develop as a critical learner you should be aware of how to recognise where you need to push your boundaries, how to do this and to set yourself criteria for doing so. You can be honest about your abilities, because only you will read your log.

---

**ACTIVITY *1.9***

*In your learning log, identify what sort of a learner you think you are and write a sentence saying why you think you fit there. You can be strategic and attribute elements of learning to different types. For example, you might be an avid reader yet do only just enough to develop what you read into an assignment. You might discount what you don't at first understand because it is too hard to pursue. You might struggle with new ideas and concepts but make a plan to include at least two in each assignment, thereby increasing your knowledge and understanding each time you write an assignment. You might seek out people who can help you if you do not understand how to improve your grades.*

---

## Comment

This should have stretched you and helped you to see that by limiting the skills in learning that you had when you joined the course you will be denying yourself any opportunities to develop your critical learning. It is not a simple thing to do but then most advances in learning are the result of sustained effort, rigorous application to detail, commitment to purpose and professional advancement.

It is generally accepted that understanding our own ways of learning, managing these so we are able to control, plan and evaluate them and consequently celebrate our achievements, gives us the confidence to survive in adversity.

---

**RESEARCH SUMMARY**

*Research has shown that students who self-manage their learning by controlling and monitoring their cognitive (developed knowledge) abilities are more able to maintain their motivation even if they are under stress or experience other distractions. This strategy is referred to as 'self-regulation' and is the opposite of 'tutor-regulation' of learning where students' learning is, to some extent, taken over by the tutor and tends to act as a de-motivating experience for students.*

*(Wolters, 1998; Pintrich and De Groot, 1990)*

---

Therefore, the posing of questions and the exposing of your personal analysis of your learning in your learning log should be seen as a liberating rather than a constraining activity. You can keep a book or file explicitly for this activity and if you are required to produce a portfolio for assessment, then excerpts can be photocopied to exemplify your learning and your attention to developing as an achievement or deep learner.

---

ACTIVITY **1.10**

*Ask yourself these questions and keep your responses in your learning log.*

1. *What do I now know about the types of questions I need to ask myself in order to promote deeper learning?*
2. *How do these questions push the boundaries of my abilities?*
3. *How might the questions I ask impact on the quality of my work?*

---

## Comment

Here are some responses from students. They had previously been working on the four question types – fundamental, connecting, hypothesis and critical question development.

Q1. What do you now know about the types of questions you need to ask yourself in order to promote deeper learning?

> Start with the questions I know the answers to and then evaluate what I know. Then go on to pose questions to myself that I don't know the answers to in order stretch myself.

> Check whether all aspects of the essay question have been covered. What do I already know and what do I need to find out? What is my opinion and why is it so? The questions asked will signal what it is to be searched for.

> Questions that can be broken down, dissected, into more manageable pieces. By answering the questions in stages and progressively asking more complicated questions, for example the four stages of the 'scaffold' of criticality (fundamental, connecting, hypothesis and critical).

> That they should lead me to analyse and think about the types of questions I ask. They should lead me to explore the meaning of the topic under discussion and stretch my abilities to think about the question. Asking myself about the 'key' questions would give me more understanding and this would help with the written work.

> The types of questions to ask are those that would promote the questioning of assumptions. These would allow for the inclusion of contrasting views and opinions. They would give the evidence with which to support arguments. If this contrasts with 'received' views, then it allows you to look at the evidence and justify your decision to sustain or change your current views and beliefs.

That the questions I ask myself should problematise my own approach and personal views to expand my own critical thinking,

I should ask those questions that allow me to focus on offering a critique. (This means evidencing several perspectives and then being able to evaluate my own position.)

Q2. *How do these questions push the boundaries of your abilities?*

By helping me to critically analyse the issues. By helping me to understand others' views. By pushing the boundaries of my existing knowledge. This means challenging myself.

By helping me to work outside my own comfort zone. Being more selective about what gets into the final version through knowing what is not relevant. By having confidence in my writing and not being afraid because I can justify and evidence my arguments.

By helping to develop new ideas and knowledge from an existing position of 'knowing' to a 'propositional' idea of considering different knowledge constructions.

Asking critical questions has made me think about how to think about a range of potential views on an issue rather than just thinking about one 'right' answer. This would help me to see some solutions. (Or maybe just lead to more questions?)

They enable you to present a balanced and evidenced argument. They change the ways in which you reflect on your learning and how you might write about this. They enable you to develop and move forward in your learning. They give you the skills to look at theories and make the connections with practice.

Gives me the possibility to look at questions in a different perspective. Perhaps one I had never considered previously or one that I had rejected.

By making me more open-minded and being able to appreciate that there are several views to most issues.

Q3. *How might the questions you ask impact on the quality of your work?*

By expanding the question set I use. By using different types of questions to improve my work.

By looking at all angles and perspectives. Also by structuring the work into known areas, potential areas of discovery and by looking at how these might lead me into new or hidden areas of enquiry.

By forming the ability to scrutinise existing knowledge and form new opinions based on evidence and reasoned arguments. This will lead to work being more structured and detailed, possessing rigour and coherence.

They should improve the written work because they will enable me to give more relevant answers. This will lead to better grades, improved structure, deeper knowledge levels, clarity of expression and to being more critical of my own work.

Asking connecting questions would help me to link my ideas to my main argument and this might help with deciding how to use coherent paragraphs to give flow and coherence to the work, whereas using fundamental questions would only prompt the most basic ideas.

By making the link between practice and theory.

Being aware of the 'ladder' approach helps me to move through the levels towards being more of a critical thinker.

By expanding the sources I use as references. By making the connections between ideas and the existing and potential new knowledge. By posing new ideas through the use of hypothetical questions. By basing judgements on evidence and posing their pros and cons.

# How can I progress through these four stages?

Using these four types of questioning techniques with yourself should lead you to aspirational learning. If you find it hard to do alone, then work with someone with whom you feel comfortable. This is not necessarily someone who is 'nice' to you but who will challenge your thinking skills.

Think about these levels too.

- **Analysis** What is being asked, assumed/implied, what is the evidence, what does it mean, how can you support/balance your argument, what are the distinctions, how have you problematised the debate?

- **Synthesis** From the evidence (re)-create, respond to the unfamiliar, combine ideas to make a new outcome, define alternatives, create a new conclusion, and propose new constructions.

- **Evaluation** How can you defend your arguments, how have you formed your judgements/evidence, does the work lead logically to a reasoned debate, are you able to expose errors in other arguments?

# Questioning and critically questioning

Most of us begin our journey in education with a very uncritical mind, yet we do question. Just think of a young child asking those questions that we find unanswerable. Why do worms taste horrible? What are the critical elements in questions and how can you come to recognise them so that they become second nature? Like riding a bicycle, asking critical questions eventually becomes automatic. Yet it takes some time to learn to balance, steer and pedal at the same time. You have to think about what action to do next. So it is with asking critical questions; you have to think through the actions initially but then suddenly you realise that you are asking these sorts of questions all the time. Even in your private life you will automatically be applying your new skills to new ways of posing questions. Also, just like riding a bicycle we usually have help to get us started. A good way to do this is to choose another person or people to help you to develop.

---

**ACTIVITY *1.11***

*Think of someone whom you can trust and ask them if they would like to work with you on developing your critical questioning skills. Of course they cannot do this without developing their own skills too!*

---

## Comment

Here are some questions you might ask them to pose to you.

> *Am I able to see others' points of view?*
>
> *Do I jump to conclusions without weighing up evidence?*
>
> *Am I a good listener?*
>
> *Can I distance myself from my personal views?*
>
> *Can I present a logical view of something?*
>
> *Do I learn from what I read?*
>
> *Have I changed my views after being convinced by the views of others?*
>
> *Am I able to contemplate several viewpoints at the same time?*
>
> *Can I think creatively?*
>
> *Can I conceptualise complex ideas?*
>
> *Am I able to deal with conflictual situations where others refute my ideas?*
>
> *Can I bear 'not knowing'?*

Here are some strategies for creating critical questions.

Asking critical questions is a practised art and needs to be based on thoughtfulness, reflection, emotional intelligence and openness. There are some strategies that might help you to create a framework within which to develop your techniques and skills.

A good way to work towards achieving these skills is to map a way forward.

You might use the FCHC (fundamental, connecting, hypothesis, critical) scaffold referred to earlier, as this will enable you to develop increasingly more complex questions to prompt a breadth and depth of criticality.

You might use a staged approach, sometimes called 'future basing'. Where do I want to be in one week's time, one month's time, one year's time?

## Example of future basing

| | Theme | What do I need to do? | What/who would help me? |
|---|---|---|---|
| **One week** | De-personalise when debating | Pose critical questions to the group/myself | Special peer/tutors |
| **One month** | Conceptualising complex ideas | Unpack ideas using spider or ripple pictures | Lateral thinking |
| **One year** | Adopt a new belief position | Question views that are different from my own | Listen to/research ideas alternative to mine |

You don't have to use a linear method as above but could be more creative. One technique is to use mind maps. These are non-linear ways of representing ideas, thoughts and actions visually. You could use colours, bold, broken, double lines, circles, squares, triangles, speech bubbles and 'clouds' to denote your stages.

See Tony Buzan's publications for examples of mind maps.

An 'objective tree' could also be used in a similar way (see Thompson and Thompson 2008, p83, for another example).

Alternatively, you might create a 'poster' of your intentions. This is an increasingly popular way of assessing students in a more creative way than the 3,000-word essay (see Figure 1.6).

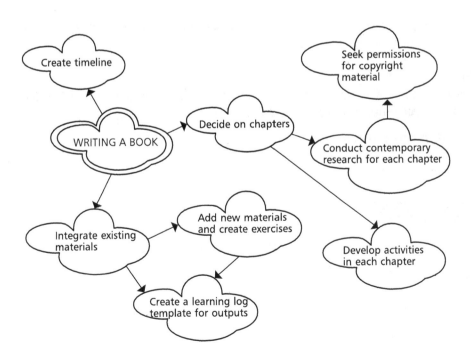

*Figure 1.4 Example of a mind map*

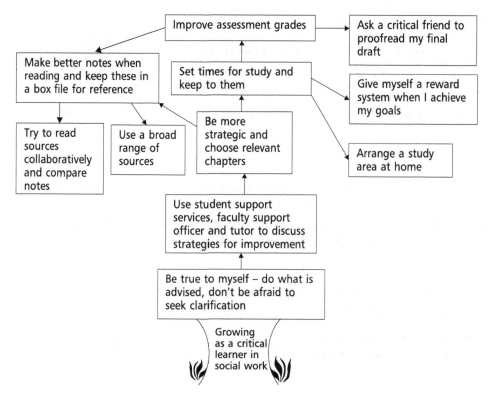

*Figure 1.5 Example of an objective tree*

These are just some ideas to promote your skills in asking critical questions. Here is another textual way that is fun to do.

### Haiku
Haiku is a form of Japanese poetry containing 17 syllables in the form of 5–7–5 represented as three lines. It is a complete poem.

> *Me, learning to learn*
> *Knowing to begin, to ask*
> *Critical questions*

---

**ACTIVITY 1.12**

*Have a go at writing your own haiku in your learning log. Try to make it representative of how you feel now about asking critical questions. It may be positive like the one above or you may still feel doubtful about your abilities as expressed here:*

Saying how I learn
Achievement, deep or surface
Unsure, let's discuss

*If you are using this book in a learning group, then share your poems with others and enjoy.*

CONTINUING PROFESSIONAL DEVELOPMENT
CPD Academic Practice

Manchester Metropolitan University

# Exploring the possibilities of teaching students the art of being critical though the use of critical questions

## CRITICAL THINKING

Knowledge
Open mindedness
Reflection
Relinquishes beliefs
Preparedness to change

Deductive skills
Reflexivity

## CRITICAL ANALYSIS

Make connections
Interrogate new ideas
Lateral and creative thinking

Present balanced arguments
Consolidate knowledge/learning
Pose unanswerable questions
Possess a world consciousness about the construction of ideas
Identify tensions

## CRITICAL EVALUATION

## RESEARCH

From analysis of BA Social Work critical learning portfolios 2005 – 6 students had:

changed their ways of reflecting
identified new thinking as a result of reflecting
developed a critical approach to own understanding of the world and to their existing knowledge
understood how the world is socially constructed
recognised ambiguities and tensions in their work
able to link theory and practice.

**Some books**
Browne M N and Keeley S J (2006) Asking the Right Questions : A Guide to Critical Thinking 8th Edn. Prentice Hall UK.
Ramsey V R. (1996) Practical Strategies for Critical Thinking Houghton Mifflin, Boston USA

**And some websites**
www.philsci.org.uk /cgi/wcritmagazine/resed.html
www.clear.unl.ca learn.com/.html
www.fromthewilderness.com/free-www3/052703_9_questions
**And one for fun.**
www.criterionmaynews.com/

### What are critical questions?

**Fundamental**
What is/are...?
Who...?
When...?
How much/many...?
What is an example of...?

**Connecting**
How...?
Why...?
What are reasons for...?
What are the functions/process of...?
What are the causes/results of...?
What are differences/similarities?
What are relationships between...?
How does...apply to...
What are conflicts/solutions?
What evidence is offered?
What other arguments are there?

**Hypothesis**
If...occurs, then what happens?
If...had happened what would be different?
What would the use of ???
Theory/ideas/methods/strategies say would happen?

**Critical Questions**
How would you evaluate issues in the debate? Are they:
Correct, effective, relevant, clear, logical, applicable, well supported, ethical or not?
What are pros and cons, advantages or disadvantages?
What might solutions be?
What is my opinion and can I support it with evidence/

### Honesty Exercise

After reading the following paragraph write down everything you know about this topic. Then organise the items into groups. (Use a concept map to help you). Ask yourself 'How are these related?' 'Could I include anything else?'

Then ask yourself 'What is the significance of all this?' 'What can it be used for?' 'What are the implications?'

'Is there anything which doesn't fit or which doesn't agree with the facts or with my personal experience?'

Edited from 'Question of the week' Guardian 23.09.06 by Matt Keating.

'Can you stay honest and keep your job?'

Being truthful has its consequences. After street protests in Budapest this week calling for his resignation, the Hungarian prime minister probably wishes he had been less frank. In a private speech that was subsequently leaked, he said that his party had screwed up and lied morning, noon and night about the state of the economy to get re-elected. The Prime Minister refused to step down. This raises the question: is honesty the best policy at work? A survey by the Institute of Directors found that UK bosses prize openness and honesty highly among their staff. These attributes could mean the difference between keeping or losing your job.

Form an argument to put your view forward, supporting it with evidence. REASONS→ CONCLUSIONS → ARGUMENT

*Figure 1.6 Example of poster presentation*

## CHAPTER SUMMARY

- This chapter has introduced you to what it means to be able to pose critical questions in order to develop your ability to obtain a greater breadth and depth in your studies. This ability is a predisposition for the following chapters on critical reading, critical writing, critical reasoning and finally to becoming a critical practitioner.
- It has explored some of the strategies necessary to be able to pose critical questions and because these are not unique to questioning techniques, many of them will be revisited in the following chapters.
- Importantly the chapter has demonstrated that the ability to pose critical questions is central to being thoughtful, considered, clear-thinking, reasoned in judgement, open-minded, logical and analytical. Some of you will already possess these attributes but for others the journey of change is just beginning. Change is to be recognised as necessary if you are to encapsulate the skills of criticality but it is not something that will happen overnight. Be prepared to make small advances and to celebrate these rather than be disillusioned when taking larger steps that don't work. We can all achieve small changes without needing to be the world's best critical advocates.
- Some strategies for making your thinking visual have been included and you should continue to use these as you work through the book. Finally, to expose your abilities as a learner I have asked you to begin to keep a learning log as you work through the activities in the book. This is not for anyone else to assess but is to enable you to see how much you have progressed.
- Having developed your critical questioning techniques you will have posed relevant and pertinent questions for yourself and will now need to begin researching what the theorists, researchers, experts, service users, carers, etc., are saying about the issue. This leads to the next chapter where the theme is 'Developing critical reading'.

**FURTHER READING**

**Cottrell, S** (2005) *Critical thinking skills*. Basingstoke: Palgrave Macmillan.

This text is about developing effective analysis and argument in order to think more critically. Part of this is the creation of argument analysis in Chapter 3. Knowing what questions to ask in order to create plausible arguments is crucial. If you enjoy quiz books and have a sense of humour, you will enjoy working through this book. It also has clear application to other chapters in this book.

**Fook, J** (2002) *Social work – critical theory and practice*. London: Sage.

This is quite a complex text with some weighty notions of the position occupied by social work. However, the questioning techniques in Chapters 7 and 8 with regard to the deconstruction and reconstruction of critical social work practice and empowerment serve as exemplars to us all in the type of critical questions that lead to growth.

**USEFUL WEBSITES**

**www.scie.org.uk**
Here you can type 'resource guides' into the search box and look at the key questions for social work education in a number of specialisms. These will show you the type of questions that are considered to be critical in social work research and practice guides.

**www.skillsforcare.org.uk**
Lists valid organisations/partner organisations

**www.scie-socialcareonline.org.uk**
Lists valid databases and electronic libraries, journals, libraries, news and websites.

**www.nationalcareforum.org.uk**
This is a forum for publications and information, discussion groups and presentations of the 'not-for-profit' sector for health and social care.

# Some possible answers to the critical questions quiz in Activity 1.3

Statement                                                    (Generally) True/False

1. Fundamental questions are those that really get to the bottom of the issue.     FALSE

*Answer.* They prompt only surface-level answers, but they do make a good starting point.

2. An hypothesis question can only result from having done lots of very     TRUE
focused reading.

*Answer.* To create a more critical answer you will need to have a deeper knowledge base of the issue, but you might begin by doing some general reading.

3. A connecting question means I would only write about two opposing     FALSE
views in the assignment.

*Answer.* Many differing perspectives should be explored in order to make links to support a view, but you might begin with two opposing views.

4. Critical questions are those that deal with emergencies of some kind.     FALSE

*Answer.* They might, but this was a joke question. 'Critical' is used in higher education to mean 'crucial' or central to an issue.

5. Fundamental questions don't stretch us to understand at deeper levels.     TRUE

*Answer.* They allow for simplistic answers that seduce us into thinking we have done a good piece of work.

6. An hypothesis question is based only on my own views.     FALSE

*Answer.* While your views might be legitimately given, scholarly learning must evidence them.

7. Asking connecting questions would help me to see alternative views.     TRUE

*Answer.* They enable links to be made and the exposure of personal bias.

8. Critical questions allow for deeper learning.     TRUE

*Answer.* They push the boundaries of knowledge and enable us to ask questions that we cannot currently answer.

9. A connecting question would enable me to demonstrate how I used     FALSE
the telephone.

*Answer.* Another joke question.

10. A fundamental question would help me in working with people who were     FALSE
experiencing mental ill health.

*Answer.* This is also a joke question, but actually it might!

11. A critical question would provoke some challenge to me by posing a question    TRUE
that I couldn't currently answer.

*Answer*. This is how we push through learning barriers to reveal new knowledge, ideas, beliefs and values.

12. An hypothesis question is one used only when completing a thesis.    FALSE

*Answer*. These questions should be used when completing any written work and when posing questions to guide and deepen learning.

How did you do?
If you spotted all the five 'TRUE' answers, well done.

If you were correct in most of the seven 'FALSE' answers, especially well done. In order to do this you would have needed to think more deeply to refute what the text was saying to you.

If you managed to see the humour in the three joke questions you are well disposed to become a critical thinker. You are able to see the literal train of thought but to recognise it for inconsequential within the argument.

# Chapter 2
## Developing critical reading

**A C H I E V I N G   A   S O C I A L   W O R K   D E G R E E**

This chapter will help you to develop the following capabilities, to the appropriate level, from the **Professional Capabilities Framework**:

- **Professionalism**
Demonstrate the importance of personal and professional boundaries.

- **Values and ethics**
Demonstrate awareness of own personal values and how these can impact on practice.

- **Knowledge**
Demonstrate an initial understanding of the range of theories and models for social work intervention.

- **Critical reflection and analysis**
Understand the roles of reflective practice and demonstrate basic skills of reflection.

- **Intervention and skills**
Demonstrate core communication skills and the capacity to develop them.

It will also introduce you to the following standards as set out in the 2008 social work subject benchmark statement:

4.2   At honours level, the study of social work involves the integrated study of subject-specific knowledge, skills and values and the critical application of research knowledge from the social and human sciences, and from social work to inform understanding and to underpin action, reflection and evaluation.

5.1.4 Social work theory.

6.6   Students should engage in a broad range of activities, including with other professionals and with service users and carers, to facilitate critical reflection. These include reading, self-directed study, research ...

## Introduction

Reading critically means reading with a critical mind. That means holding in your mind as you read questions such as: who has written this, for what audience, does the piece have depth and breadth, does it perpetuate or refute potentially discriminatory ideas, does it use sound evidence and research that possesses integrity, and is it rigorous in examining all the issues?

A good critical reader is able to differentiate between texts in order to make comparisons and to appreciate the validity of an argument presented by an author with whom they disagree. It can be more difficult to open yourself up to arguments that hold an oppositional stance to your own, yet this is a good way in which to consolidate your position.

By the end of this chapter you will be able to:

- make judgements about how to read more critically;
- create your own rubric (template) to apply to your reading;
- use a glossary of words to use through the stages in reading critically;
- use annotation to develop your critical reading ability.

# What is critical reading?

When we read critically we make judgements about:

- how the text has been written;
- what the central argument is;
- what position the author takes;
- how the issues raised might connect with broader contexts.

It is useful to read through once first to get a grasp of the content and then read again with these critical questions in mind.

Critical reading is:

> *Reading to evaluate un-stated assumptions and biases consciously identifying patterns of language and content and their interrelationships.*

(Daniel J. Kurland, www.criticalreading.com, accessed 18 April 2008)

This definition implies that reading is undertaken while holding in mind a large basket containing critical elements. These elements – unstated assumptions, biases, patterns of language and their interrelationships – go beyond the generic definition of reading to denote that:

> *Critical reading is a more complex definition applied to discipline specific contexts, to complex learning and to the mood of the writer and the mood we are in whilst reading.*

(Daniel J. Kurland, www.criticalreading.com, accessed 18 April 2008)

---

**ACTIVITY 2.1**

*Read this newspaper article about student loans.*

**Money troubles**

*So 'giving students from poor families significant sums of money at the beginning of the academic year could be asking for trouble' (News, 7 April). What patronising arrogance. The article stated 'these students might be sons helping their single parents to pay off*

*Continued*

---

*debts or minority ethnic students using their loans to contribute to the family business'. So much worse of course than students not from 'poor families' who spend their money on beer, clubbing, cannabis and other things that make up the so-called student lifestyle.*

*Sadie Williams – Lancaster University*

*Reprinted with the author's permission and by kind permission of*

Times Higher Education, 5 May 2006

## Comment

Before you considered a university education you probably would have glanced at the item and thought it was rather elitist, that it didn't mean anything to you and you would not have pursued it.

As a university student yourself you would be drawn by the title as the issue of student debt means that most will be working in addition to studying. You might even think that the article will tell you something about where you can get help with debt or grants to help you out. So the title of the article might draw you in.

You begin to see the significance of the inverted commas used extensively – that they point you to some other comments made and with which the author is taking issue. So the inclusion of these allows the current author to take an oppositional stance – to oppose what the original writer said. However, this author does not state this in the text but instead takes an ironic position and implies their irony by using a stereotype of what 'students' are like.

It is useful to have a set of questions ready that you can apply to your reading. In this example you might have used the following to read the article critically.

Who is the audience?

What are the main claims?

What is the position of the author?

Are the points and arguments well developed?

Is the argument deep or surface level?

Do I agree or refute it and why?

How would I evaluate the content?

In what context is the writer making these claims?

Is the evidence convincing; how would I evaluate it?

---

ACTIVITY **2.2**

*Write your responses to these questions now and put them into your learning log. Use the questions given above to guide your responses. Put a heading 'Critical reading' and the activity number then write each critical question with your answer underneath it.*

*Just think if you were to write up to 300 words for each. By the end you will probably have written a 2,700-word critique of the article.*

---

## Comment

You should be thinking about the following.

What sort of person reads this newspaper and why? Would students be likely to read it or would it be academics, parents, or government officials? As it is such a short and snappy article, does it have more impact than a lengthy one? What is the impact of the style used? Would it be useful to adopt the same style?

Does the style leave assumptions to be made about the claims it makes? What do I assume the writer is saying? Might there be other messages here?

What has happened recently to prompt the writer to send this article? There is usually a catalyst (trigger), such as a government minister's speech or a development in the news causing a writer to feel strongly enough make the effort to do something out of the ordinary.

What deductive (from general ideas to specific understanding) elements can I identify as contributing to my understanding? For example, there is a number of clues about what the writer thinks, and there are quotes from a writer with an alternative view.

What does the language used tell you about the writers? Do you think the writer of this article is a student, a parent, a lecturer, someone from student support services, a bank manager? Whatever, both authors seem to think that students do spend their loans in areas not normally associated with learning. Is this legitimate in your view?

Does the article convince you that there are certain ways for students to spend money that would strongly contribute to a student's ability to concentrate on their learning? Alternatively, do students expect to sample freedom in using their loans to join in a student lifestyle (whatever that is?) when they go to university? Can you evaluate the differing perspectives of students, parents, etc.?

What would be your personal view of both the article and your analysis of how students manage their loans?

Don't forget to give your evidence and then examine it to test if you think it is robust. It is useful to work with a learning mentor or critical friend on this exercise.

You can find several examples of 'tools' to help with critical reading on the web. However, I always feel I work better with something I have created for myself. Let's move on to look at one of these tools or rubrics that you might use with your critical reading.

# Creating your own rubric for critical reading

Again using the 'Money troubles' text, visualise your analysis of the text by creating a rubric (a plan or set of instructions) against which you can indicate your initial feelings about it, as in Figure 2.1. This will be useful to point you in the direction you need to go to make a deeper scrutiny of the issues under debate.

An example of this would be to put a list of headings as follows.

|  | Clearly identified | Unclear | Not sure |
|---|---|---|---|
| Who is the audience? | Funders/tax payers | Parents | Students |
| What are the main claims? | Students from poor households should not be treated detrimentally in loan allocation. | Critics from richer households should not think they can judge those less fortunate. | Students must be held to account about how they spend their loans. |
| How would I evaluate the content? | There is a moral issue in how students choose to spend their loans. | | |
| And so on ... | | | |

*Figure 2.1  Rubric development*

Might this help you to dissect the article more critically? Would you find it difficult to put something under each heading? Could you do this activity in about an hour? The idea is to keep your responses concise and focused rather than going into lengthy explanations. This skill will help you when we come to the next chapter on developing critical writing.

Stella Cottrell gives more examples of methods of recording critical notes for 'analysing arguments' and 'making concise critical notes' in her book *Critical thinking skills* (Cottrell, 2005, pp155–7). She includes looking for flaws and gaps, strengths and weaknesses, comparisons with other authors and whether the conclusions are grounded in the content.

# Focusing, selecting and weighing up evidence

Authors on critical reading advise that it is better to skim-read and take in the introduction and conclusion before concentrating on the whole article. This gives you clues as to the content and prompts your own thinking about what position you might hold.

---

**ACTIVITY 2.3**

*Read this example of a student writing about her practice.*

> *This account examines some of the assumptions I made while conducting an interview with a prospective volunteer who was applying to help in my placement. I was assisted in my reflection of the incident by my practice teacher, and through this was able to realise how I had been oppressive and discriminatory in my approach.*

*Continued*

---

*The interviewee was a 56-year-old white woman who was unmarried. She had difficulty walking due to a severe car accident some years ago and had to take strong medication for this and other conditions. She was overbearing in her approach, telling me how good she was in her previous employments, yet she had not stayed long at any of them. She stated that she didn't want to work in a miserable team and that people who had degrees were often 'thick' and degrees meant nothing. It is easy for us to see how she could upset people by voicing these views with our service users. I felt she had poor 'people skills' and she would not fit well into the team. She seemed indifferent as to whether she got the position and I felt she was taking over the interview. How could I allow this person to have access to our vulnerable service users? She might at least upset people and at worst exacerbate their mental health condition.*

*As this was one of my 'observed practice' assessments I met with my practice teacher for supervision shortly afterwards. I was shocked by her interpretation of the event. She said that I had taken over the interview, had questioned the woman more than other candidates and had failed to delve more deeply into some of her answers. This had not allowed her to explain her perspective, i.e. that she was a long-term carer for her mother who has Alzheimer's disease and that she has no qualifications because she was the family breadwinner due to her father's early death.*

*My practice teacher was able to help me to see that, with appropriate training, an accepting attitude and a recognition of the interviewee's personal and social circumstances, she could become a valued supporter for people receiving our mental health service.*

*In conclusion, I found the whole experience very difficult because I was so sure that I had practised very well and had been careful to protect our service users. In fact I had failed to recognise the potential of the woman in helping and what she could bring as a disadvantaged person herself. I saw that I allowed my likes and dislikes to influence me in the interview and that there was a mindset that I needed to change. I began by asking my practice teacher to help me with some strategies to change my attitude. I now recognise the power that my own attitudes can have by insidiously infiltrating into my values, beliefs and therefore my practice.*

*(Student narrative of practice 2004 – contained in Jones, S (2006) Growing critical thinkers in the social work profession – paper given at the SWAP conference – Swansea)*

## Comment

In reading the introduction and conclusion you will see that the central claims for the article are now evident to you.

The context is a volunteer interview, in which the student social worker makes assumptions that turn out to be incorrect but which influence her practice negatively. The consequences cause her to seek help from her practice teacher in developing some strategies for change in recognising how she might deal with her negative attitudes and potential abuse of power. Now you can skim-read the middle paragraphs to find out more about the context and issues that arose.

The student thought she had conducted the interview well and gave evidence to show how unfit the candidate was to work in the organisation. She mentioned how she felt about the candidate and deduced that she would not be an appropriate worker. The student was shocked by her practice teacher's response that exposed the former's discriminatory practice. Eventually the student asked her practice teacher to help her to develop some strategies in order that she would not make the same mistake again.

What elements would you select for your 'critical reading'?

You might unpack the evidence that the student social worker gives for her assumptions and, like the practice teacher, refute this as a reason to deny the candidate the opportunity to help others. You should also identify with the alternative, the student perspective, and be able to juxtapose these (show how you appreciate them both).

You could interpret why you think she felt the need to protect service users from this candidate and judge what was presented as fact, values, beliefs or opinions. In order to do this you could take actual and inferred understandings. For example, she states that *she was overbearing in her approach*.

You will infer what you think she meant by this. Was she speaking too loudly, butting in and using body language to dominate? Or was she nervous and speaking too quickly, jumping in, too eager to give the right answer? Perhaps she was leaning forward and looking intently at the student because she had a hearing loss.

How might you weight the evidence presented by the student?

The student recognised the use of the word 'thick' when referring to people who have a degree as a red rag to a bull. She was studying hard in difficult home circumstances herself and felt that this portrayed an attitude that denounced all her own efforts to gain her degree. So words themselves and consequently language have a powerful influence on how we critically read. You might therefore choose to focus on the language the student uses to articulate her argument (to critically discuss and evidence her position).

Finally, you will come to some position yourself on her ability to critically reflect on her practice. Was she a good reflective practitioner or not?

Yet there is more to critical analysis than this. There is a deeper and more critical way to read this account. What the guidance above does is to show you that you can employ strategies that will lead you to be more critical in your reading. However, in order to use these skills at a much deeper level you will be examining the content, language and structure using a 'helicopter' view. This means expanding the wider possibilities of knowledge applications while holding on to the central themes.

So when the student speaks of interviewing volunteers you will be making a note to explore research conducted on this subject. Similarly, as the student asks her practice teacher to help her to develop some strategies, you will be thinking what those might be and where you could find out more about them. The ripple diagram in Figure 2.1 shows the 'stakeholders' (interested parties) who should be contributing to your evaluation.

By taking these different stakeholder perspectives you will demonstrate a considered view in analysing the impact they might have on the student's position. It may seem to you that the management committee, or mental health discourse has nothing to do with the student account. However, if you can show that you understand how the student narrative sits within a much wider context of accountability and anti-oppressive practice you will be showing how you are moving to deeper levels of analysis rather than accepting the surface level account of one student. Ripple diagrams are a good way to visualise this.

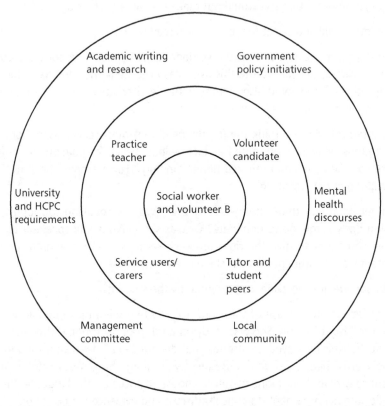

*Figure 2.2 Ripple diagram of student connectedness to broader societal influences*

A three-step guide to critical reading is to ask yourself these preliminary questions.

- What does the text say – what information is imparted and what knowledge do I gain from it?

- What does the text do – what concerns and implications does it raise for me?

- What does it mean – how does it stretch my thinking about the topic?

These questions will draw you into a deeper reading of the text but will also flag up questions that you are not yet able to answer. These should be logged too and used in professional development group discussions and in tutorials with your tutor and practice teacher.

In order to judge the authenticity of texts and to what extent writers try to persuade, to convince us that their perception is right, and to offer reasons why we should believe them, we can use some techniques that allow us to delve into the deeper aspects of language. We could say we can 'excavate' the language of texts by examining what linguistic techniques are being used.

# The language of critical reading

Eventually, critical readers are able to analyse the various parts of a text without thinking too much about what it is they are doing. This is because they have developed a system that recognises what is 'critical' about their reading. Here are some terms that you need to know so that you can begin to integrate them into your study skills.

I have included some examples of the words exemplified by referring back to Activity 2.3.

| | |
|---|---|
| **Context** | the circumstances under which the text was written, e.g. a student social worker on placement under assessment in one of her formal observations. |
| **Premise** | the supporting claims in an argument, e.g. the reasons she gave in taking action to change her behaviour. |
| **Hypothesis** | a tentative explanation for something, e.g. the student's recognition of her own oppressive and discriminatory behaviour. |
| **Argument** | one or more premises given in support of a conclusion, e.g. failure to recognise the woman's potential, to understand how the woman's experiences might offer empathy to service users and the need to recognise her own (student's) bias. |
| **Deductive reasoning** | drawing one conclusion from many positions, e.g. the student's critique of her own practice leads you to conclude that she is a reflective practitioner. |
| **Inductive reasoning** | taking one idea and expanding to consider all the implications. As this was a formal observed practice you can infer that she would have been nervous, keen to do the 'right thing', aware that it would influence her final assessment, impact on the agency view of her and be considered by a practice panel reading her practice teacher assessment of her, so therefore open to wider stakeholder scrutiny. |
| **Corollary** | a statement that is easily proved by reference to another, e.g. the volunteer was forceful in the interview, therefore the student felt she was not a fit person to work with service users. This might be a false corollary as the perception of the student might be flawed. |
| **Assertion** | a statement that is easily proved by reference to another, e.g. the student asserts that she needs to change her mindset in order to recognise her own discriminatory practice. |

| | |
|---|---|
| **Reasoning** | logical thinking in order to get results or reach a conclusion, e.g. the student asks her practice teacher to help her with some strategies to change entrenched attitudes. |
| **Opinion** | a view of something based on personal judgement, e.g. the student's opinion of the candidate was that she was unfit to become a volunteer at the centre. |
| **Fact** | the truth backed by evidence that something has happened or will happen or a statistic demonstrated by evidence, e.g. the student's performance in the interview would be recorded and used in her practice teacher report. |
| **Logic** | distinguishing between good and bad reasoning used to form a view or conclusion about something, e.g. the student's view of the volunteer was not logical because she had allowed her own bias to interfere with her deduction. The practice teacher pointed out a logical progression that would support the volunteer in becoming an asset to the organisation. |
| **Rhetoric** | persuasive techniques used to convince the reader, often sounding pompous, e.g. the student says how could she let this woman have access to vulnerable service users? |
| **Structure** | the flow of the article sets the intention, leads the discussion logically and ends with a coherent conclusion, e.g. the student leads us through a journey of action, thoughts, reflection and uses these to explain her new position. |
| **Consistency** | the focus remains constant and does not go off at a tangent, e.g. the student narrative is consistent with her reflection on the experience of the interview. |
| **Assumption** | believed to be true but without proof, e.g. the student made assumptions about the volunteer's abilities as a support worker through her perception of how she behaved in the interview but she did not account for her own bias in her interpretation. |
| **Stereotype** | an oversimplified view of one or a group held by another or group of others, e.g. the student was unable to see the individuality or the potential of the volunteer because she perceived her as a disabled person with attitude. This is often a perception given to disabled people when they are vocal about their rights to equality. |
| **Comparison** | being able to see differing views while recognising their strengths and weaknesses, e.g. the student was able to consider her attitude towards the volunteer during the process of the interview, through reflection over the weekend and after discussion with her practice teacher. |
| **Complicity** | using words and phrases that assume we all agree with the writer, e.g. the student states *It is easy for us to see …* This draws the |

reader into agreement and seduces us to agree with the writer's comments and ultimately their attitudes.

**Theory**

rules, ideas, principles and techniques that have been developed distinct from practice but are to be applied in practice, e.g. the student could have used Kolb's reflective cycle theory to explain her journey in that she had used some concrete experience as a basis for her change strategies.

**Critical sources**

these are texts (or erudite individuals) that are considered to be authoritative within your discipline area, e.g. the student sees her practice teacher as an authoritative person to help her to develop strategies for change.

Her practice teacher may recommend appropriate reading and the student could be referred to credible internet resources, research and her tutor. The Joe Bloggs webpage on 'how to be nice and help people' is unlikely to be a credible source.

**Validity**

the work is sound and defensible, e.g. it is the student's own work based on an actual placement event about which she can reason.

**Propositions**

e.g. why the student considered that the volunteer was unsuitable for her agency. In this case her propositions were unfounded and probably untrue.

Now how about another quiz? Let's play 'Twenty questions'. You will be encountering the words in the glossary above. Have a look at the following extract from Lymbery and Postle (2007) and the ensuing statements. Which answer most closely represents the statements? You have to be careful because in some both answers may be correct.

### Social work in Britain

*The future of social work in the context of British society is hard to predict. Social workers will need to accept, and adjust to, periods of intense change in the organisation and management of their work. Practitioners must therefore retain clarity about their role and contribution to welfare services and be prepared to argue for the continuing relevance of their role within environments that they may find harsh and unforgiving. The fundamental changes that have been set in train for social work education confirm the fact that social workers must simultaneously operate in ways that deliver a good quality of service, while also being prepared to amend their practice in accordance with frequent adjustments to their organisational locations.*

*Although this appears a daunting task, this book argues that it is achievable. However, we are not underestimating the task's intensity, scale or complexity: rather, we suggest that in order to accomplish it practitioners need to identify and adhere to key tenets of social work that have been neglected in recent years. In this way, we can start to transform social work practice and its education. The starting point lies in recognising the breadth of the social work task, well captured in the International Federation of Social Workers' (IFSW) definition of social work, which suggests that it should not be limited to the narrow discharge of statutory functions that has characterised its recent history in the UK.*

(Lymbery and Postle, 2007, p3)

---

### ACTIVITY 2.4

*Now answer the following.*

1. *The context in which the book was written is*
   - (a)   *Britain*
   - (b)   *uncertainty.*
2. *One premise supporting the argument is*
   - (a)   *periods of intense change in the organisation and management of work*
   - (b)   *practitioners must be clear about their role.*
3. *The authors' hypothesis is*
   - (a)   *that in order to flourish as professional social workers in the future, we need to revisit previous key fundamental beliefs*
   - (b)   *that to survive, social work must change.*
4. *The central argument of the piece is*
   - (a)   *life is going to get harder for social workers*
   - (b)   *in order to survive change, social work will need to incorporate some old ideas into new thinking.*
5. *We can deduce that*
   - (a)   *social work education needs to be transformed*
   - (b)   *It isn't possible to predict the future of social work in Britain.*
6. *We can infer that*
   - (a)   *there will be a movement away from a tick-box approach to risk*
   - (b)   *more traditional strategies will gain favour within the social care field.*
7. *A corollary to retaining clarity of the role of social work is*
   - (a)   *the ability of social workers to argue for their continuing place within difficult environments whilst offering good quality provision*
   - (b)   *that social work is a daunting task.*
8. *The writers make an assertion when they say that*
   - (a)   *the future context of social work in Britain is hard to predict*
   - (b)   *social workers operate in ways that deliver good quality services.*
9. *Good reasoning is demonstrated by*
   - (a)   *recognising that change is achievable*
   - (b)   *recognising that although the task is daunting there are suggestions as to how social work can be transformed.*
10. *It is the authors' opinion that*
    - (a)   *social work promotes change and problem-solving*
    - (b)   *practitioners need to identify with some neglected areas of social work practice.*
11. *There is a factual definition of*
    - (a)   *what social work should be*
    - (b)   *what it should not be.*

*Continued*

ACTIVITY **2.4** *Continued*

12. The text gives a logical explanation of
    (a) how social work needs to change
    (b) what theory would be important.
13. The use of rhetoric can be seen by
    (a) a suggestion that social workers must retain clarity about their contribution to services
    (b) a suggestion that recently social work has been limited to a narrow discharge of statutory functions.
14. The authors lead us incrementally through their arguments by
    (a) complaining about how social work is not fit for purpose
    (b) stating a position then saying how it could be achieved.
15. The views are not consistent with
    (a) an academic perception of social work in Britain
    (b) an explanation of the value of current-day social work practice.
16. The authors make assumptions about
    (a) what the reader knows about the context of social work in Britain today
    (b) the nature of the social work task.
17. The article gives the impression that stereotypes exist by suggesting that
    (a) all social work is in crisis
    (b) social workers frequently move a lot.
18. The authors make comparisons by
    (a) underestimating the intensity of change
    (b) saying how weaknesses can be dealt with.
19. The authors make us complicit in their beliefs by
    (a) using 'we' when referring to transforming social work practice
    (b) arguing that this change is achievable.
20. The authors' general proposition is
    (a) that recently social work has only been about discharging narrow statutory functions
    (b) that the breadth of the social work task as stated by the IFSW is a good starting point for change.

Check your answers to the Twenty questions quiz with those given at the end of the chapter.

Include your answers in your learning log and reflect on what you learned in doing this activity.

## Comment

This is not an easy quiz and you will have had to do lots of deep thinking about these questions. In some ways it is the process of thinking about what you are reading that is more important than the outcome – what you now believe. If you are able to use your reading to develop a good ability to defend your thought processes you will be able to create persuasive arguments in your written work and in debate with others. So it really doesn't matter whether you got the answers right, it is the fact that you processed the information and came to a conclusion that is important. One way to help you to analyse and dissect your reading is to use annotation.

# Using annotation

Some students find it very helpful to annotate a text and add their own notes. You might begin by using a system of highlighting the text. For example, you could use different colours or shapes to select text that you:

- think is the central argument of the piece;
- tells you something about the author, the context or the purpose of the piece;
- agree or disagree with and have evidence to support this;
- need to explore further as it is new to you;
- don't understand and need to refer back to.

---

**ACTIVITY 2.5**

**Using annotation to focus your critical reading**

*The following phrases (I have given them numbers) are taken from Chapter 2, 'The critical challenges for social work' in Social work: Critical theory and practice (Fook 2002, p4). Your possible annotations are shown beneath each phrase.*

1. What is particularly interesting about our foregoing post-modern analysis is that it does not function as a totalising analysis.

*Perhaps this means that post-modernism [check what the actual definition of this is] cannot be applied as a blanket analysis. That it cannot have one explanation or application to everything. I agree with this because I think immigration has both negative and positive aspects in the UK.*

2. It points up many types of contradictions in the current state of affairs.

*Yes I was thinking about using crops for fuel and thought what a good thing to use vacant land for growing seeds from which oil can be extracted. Then I saw how suddenly the price of everything seemed to increase, fuel, rice, flour, bread and how this impacted on the poor most of all! That was because instead of using land to grow crops to feed people, it is now being used to grow oil crops for transport fuel.*

3. For instance, globalisation can be seen as responsible for greater unifying and compressing of differences on the one hand, and on the other for a greater social fragmentation.

*I think the laws in different countries seem to be coming to more agreement but there are greater gaps between rich and poor. Not sure I understand this so do some research.*

*Continued*

**ACTIVITY 2.5** *Continued*

4. It creates new exclusions at the same time as it opens up possibilities for differences.

*I suppose I could bring in the EU and Polish workers here and the new law to make some immigrants pay high prices to come to the UK. More research on this as I heard that immigrants with skills that we needed would be allowed in.*

5. Even in the more immediate field of professional practice, there are clear tensions between increasing managerial 'scientist' regulation and a growing culture which recognises more personal and holistic ways of understanding experience.

*Mmmm? Might this mean using the tick-box approach compared with the more humanist approaches like narrative and solution-focused work, really taking the time to understand people?*

## Comment

This model will help you to begin to compose your responses to what you are reading. You would begin with an explanation of the central arguments, why the author is stating them at this time, and what you think the article purports (intends) to do. You can then go on to select your own arguments as to why you would support or refute their contentions. You would give your own evidence for this and finally show how you are coming to understand new debates introduced by the article after researching the topics that you found difficult to understand. We will go into the skills of critical writing in the next chapter.

You will also be using critical listening skills as you are taking your notes in lectures. As you are listening, try to think not only about what is being said, but also what the alternatives might be and how you might begin to think about these things. Write these as your annotations on the lecture notes.

You can use this technique in annotating all sorts of information. What about the 'critical reading' of poems, photographs, television or radio programmes and films?

What do you think are the critical messages of this poem, 'Listen to my hands', by the author of this book?

**ACTIVITY 2.6**

**Listen to my hands**
**Sue Jones**

*When I was young and my friend*
*made movements with her mouth to spur her mother into action*
*I thought, 'how strange.'*

*Continued*

*Whilst at school and using my hands to*
*tell my friends about an exciting adventure, only to be punished*
*I thought, 'how unfair.'*

*When joining college and at lectures*
*having eyes only for my interpreter, whose presence brought me ridicule*
*I thought, 'how outrageous.'*

*When entering working life with hands fully occupied*
*in making things for those who hear and by that activity preventing my communication*
*I thought, 'how oppressive.'*

*When becoming politically active within Deaf power and consciousness movements and*
*learning to value my language and heritage that hearing people cannot access*
*I thought, 'how sad.'*

*Now recognising my value, hope for the future and equality*
*I know there is a positive future for those who do not hear or use words*
*I think, 'emancipation.'*

## Comment

(Politically signing Deaf people use a capital 'D' because they identify as an oppressed group with a shared culture and history. This does not apply to deaf children who have not yet made that choice.) In these lines the poet is writing as a deaf person. She is saying that while growing up a deaf child is confused about who they are because their world is mainly populated by hearing people who cannot communicate. Explaining something exciting using signing is often seen as being aggressive because of the large motor movements. Sometimes services put in to help seem to make matters worse because they single people out as different, when the important thing is to belong and be the same. Suddenly, when one is able to reason more as an adult, new perspectives become available and these help to reframe and recreate the experiences. Eventually this young person has become an activist for other Deaf people. This goes against the general perception of how signing Deaf people should be, i.e. compliant, uncomplaining and grateful for what they receive. To go against these received ideas is to be 'difficult', 'awkward' and a 'problem'. Instead we might see her defiance as 'spirited', 'lively' and 'refreshing', boding well for the future reform of social care provision for Deaf people who will challenge the status quo. She does all this by showing a journey from childhood to adulthood. Is the journey a metaphor for challenge?

In this age of quick access to information it is all too easy to click on a website and not question the validity of what we are reading. Try to have a list of questions in your mind as you are researching on the net. Here are some examples.

- Is this a reputable website?
- Who is controlling this information?
- Might there be a hidden agenda?

*48*

If these apply, it doesn't mean you can't use the site, but do so with caution. For example, many students use Wikipedia, but check the information by following other leads too.

---

ACTIVITY **2.7**

*Check the following on the web and then write your own annotations on them. Choose one aspect of the site to focus on.*

*Photographs*
*www.noodletools.com/debbie/literacies/visual/diglitnews.pdf*

*Films*
*www.rottentomatoes.com – Look at the reviews of the latest films.*

*TV and radio*
*www.bbc.co.uk – Enter 'tv and radio critique' into the 'search box'.*

---

## Comment

You will have found many opinions, judgements and viewpoints here, but how do you know what to believe? The best position to hold is probably one of gentle scepticism. For example, rottentomatoes.com awards ratings of films by giving ripe, squashed or new-pick tomatoes. However, the views of the film critics, who make a living out of being controversial, may be more sensational than those of the general public who just want to pass on their experience of seeing a film. That is why you need to know how the writer is constructed in order to judge whether their opinions are valid. Many quite erudite texts used in the people professions fail to identify who they are in the real sense of race, disability, class, sexuality, beliefs, culture, age and meaningful experience.

## Is all text equal?

In searching through some of the material in Activity 2.7 you should be beginning to realise that not all text carries the same weight in terms of critical reading. You may even have realised that you are focusing more quickly on text that is more meaningful to you. You may automatically be skipping over the more 'descriptive' elements and dwelling longer on those parts that expose opinions, open you up to broader debates or pose questions that you currently don't know the answers to.

Figure 2.3 (on page 54) is a model I created to develop critical reading in a group activity with students. It might be useful to ask your tutor if you can use this in one of your group sessions. The model uses critical deductive and inductive reasoning to form a holistic approach to textual analysis.

## CHAPTER SUMMARY

- Chapter 2 has built upon your critical questioning ability and given you techniques to develop your critical reading skills. In doing this you will notice that the activities and examples have begun to expose some of the difficulties of inference and subjectivity that we, as human agents, bring to our analysis. Your reflections in your learning log will act as affirmation of what you are doing well and as a repository for those unanswerable questions that 'niggle' at our consciousness. It is important that you complete these activities and record them in your log if you are to gain the most benefit from this book. You can also include these in your portfolio of learning that may be required by your social work programme. Remember that reading critically means that you excavate all the possible connections between the reading matter and broader social, economic, political, cultural and, where possible, philosophical issues.

- The importance of this chapter has been to show you the part played by rigorously evidencing your impressions while reading critically. This is the difference between merely reading and accepting and then describing. A good foundation in critical reading leads to an enhanced ability to order and shape your ideas with depth; a crucial skill in enabling you to develop as a critical writer, further discussed in the next chapter.

**My haiku**
Reading, with focus.
Exploring the construction
of knowledge and truth.

## ACTIVITY 2.8

*Write your own critical reading haiku.*

**FURTHER READING**

**Cottrell, S** (2005) *Critical thinking skills.* Basingstoke: Palgrave Macmillan.

Chapter 9 is entirely devoted to critical reading and note-making and weaves this around some practical preparation and theory interpretation as argument identification. This is very useful to get you into the habit of analysing what you read. There are some really helpful templates for you to use on pages 155–160.

**Knott, C and Scragg, T** (2007) *Reflective practice in social work.* Exeter: Learning Matters.

Chapter 4 'Reflecting as a catalyst for change' has some useful tools that can be adapted for use in critical reading. There is helpful advice on the structure of a reflective journal and some self-assessment tools. Have you thought about using a SWOT (strengths, weaknesses, opportunities and threats) analysis to help with judging what you are reading?

**USEFUL WEBSITES**

**www.rottentomatoes.com**

Look at the reviews of the latest films and decide who to believe and why. Those who are paid to write reviews need to be more sensational in their text than customers who pay to see the films.

# Twenty questions quiz – some possible answers shown in italics

1. The context in which the book was written is

   (a) Britain
   (b) *uncertainty*.

Just a little trick question there as you had to understand the meaning and not only the word 'context'.

2. One premise supporting the argument is

   (a) periods of intense change in the organisation and management of work
   (b) *practitioners must be clear about their role*.

This supports the claim that they will be better able to argue for a transformation of services.

3. The authors' hypothesis is

   (a) *that in order to proliferate as professional social workers in the future we need to revisit previous key fundamental beliefs*
   (b) that to survive, social work must change.

You could say that (b) is also partly a hypothetical view but it is not as scholarly as (a).

4. The central argument of the piece is

   (a) life is going to get harder for social workers
   (b) *new thinking will incorporate some fundamental ideas that have recently been lost and enable social work to survive change.*

The authors are suggesting that social work needs to revisit its roots to reclaim a transformational element. Maybe they are thinking of radical and community social work?

5. We can deduce that

   (a) *social work education needs to be transformed*
   (b) *it isn't possible to predict the future of social work in Britain*.

Both these statements could be deduced from the broader premises in the text: that there will be intense change, that social workers will need to argue for their role to continue, that the future will be hard to predict and that they will need to adapt their practice.

6. We can infer that

   (a) *there will be a movement away from a tick-box approach to risk*
   (b) social work agencies will move around a lot.

A tick-box approach to risk is what is often used within a narrow definition of statutory functionalism. So you could think that the piece is optimistic by broadening out the social work task.

7. A corollary to retaining clarity of the role of social work is

    (a) *the ability of social workers to argue for their continuing place within difficult environments while offering good quality provision*

    (b) that social work is a daunting task.

This means that in doing (a), social workers will be clear about their role.

8. The writers make an assertion when they say that

    (a) social workers will be required to locate in different agencies

    (b) *the future context of social work in Britain is hard to predict.*

An assertion usually means that authors are strongly assertive about what they say. It implies something more strongly meant than a statement or comment.

9. Good reasoning is demonstrated by

    (a) recognising that change is achievable

    (b) *recognising that although the task is daunting there are suggestions as to how social work can be transformed.*

Here reasons are given to show how it is demonstrated.

10. It is the authors' opinion that

    (a) social work promotes change and problem-solving

    (b) *practitioners need to identify with some neglected areas of social work practice.*

They may agree with (a) – most social workers do – but there is no evidence in this passage.

11. There is a factual definition of

    (a) what social work should be

    (b) *what it should not be.*

Although the text mentions recognising the breadth of the task, it does not say what that is. It does, however, say that social work should not be limited and narrow.

12. The text gives a logical explanation of

    (a) how social work needs to change

    (b) what theory would be important.

Neither of these because the text says how 'social workers' rather than 'social work' needs to change. Did that catch you out? It just shows how we try to make the text fit what we want to know.

13. The use of rhetoric can be seen by

    (a) a suggestion that social workers must retain clarity about their contribution to services

    (b) *a suggestion that recently social work has been limited to a narrow discharge of statutory functions.*

The authors use the words *limited to a narrow discharge of statutory functions* to convince us that current-day social work has become the job of a functionary who merely follows rules and forms.

14. The authors lead us incrementally through their arguments by

    (a) complaining about how social work is not fit for purpose
    (b) *stating a position then saying how it could be achieved*.

They suggest what the position is, what needs to be done and how that can be achieved.

15. Their views are not consistent with

    (a) an academic perception of social work in Britain
    (b) *an explanation of the value of current-day social work practice*.

The authors set out to write an academic book that says practice has to change and then go about saying how. Their focus is on transformational or aspirational social work and not on a dissection of current social work practice.

16. The authors make assumptions about

    (a) *what the reader knows about the context of social work in Britain today*
    (b) the nature of the social work task.

The main assumption is that social work is experienced by practitioners as narrow and functionalist. This may not be true in all social work fields.

17. The article gives the impression that stereotypes exist by suggesting that

    (a) *all social work is in crisis*
    (b) social workers frequently move a lot.

This may not be so for all agencies or practitioners.

18. The authors make comparisons by

    (a) saying how weaknesses can be dealt with
    (b) *linking neglected but fundamental areas in social work with the intensity and complexity of change*.

There is some notion that previous social work practice operated from a much broader basis that was more able to deal with complex social problems.

19. The authors make us complicit in their beliefs by

    (a) *using 'we' when referring to transforming social work practice*
    (b) arguing that this change is achievable.

They are drawing us in to convince us that their view is to be agreed with.

20. The authors' general proposition is

    (a) that recently social work has only been about discharging narrow statutory functions
    (b) *that the breadth of the social work task as stated by the IFSW is a good starting point for change*.

This statement sets the basis for the rest of their book in which key debates for the new foundation of social work practice are established.

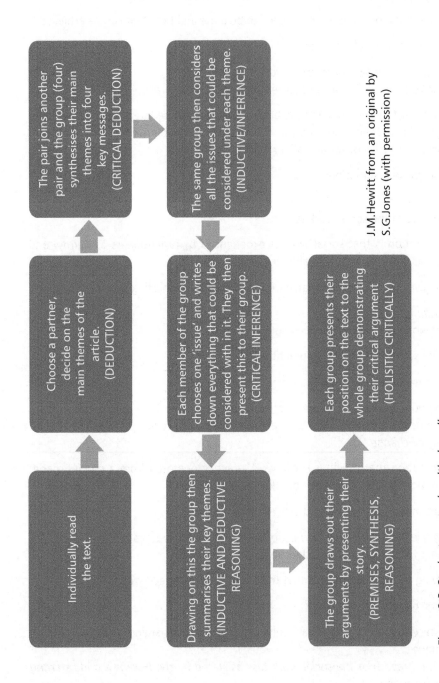

Individually read the text.

Choose a partner, decide on the main themes of the article. (DEDUCTION)

The pair joins another pair and the group (four) synthesises their main themes into four key messages. (CRITICAL DEDUCTION)

The same group then considers all the issues that could be considered under each theme. (INDUCTIVE/INFERENCE)

Each member of the group chooses one 'issue' and writes down everything that could be considered with in it. They then present this to their group. (CRITICAL INFERENCE)

Drawing on this the group then summarises their key themes. (INDUCTIVE AND DEDUCTIVE REASONING)

The group draws out their arguments by presenting their story. (PREMISES, SYNTHESIS, REASONING)

Each group presents their position on the text to the whole group demonstrating their critical argument (HOLISTIC CRITICALLY)

J.M.Hewitt from an original by S.G.Jones (with permission)

*Figure 2.3 Student agency in critical reading*

# Chapter 3
## Developing critical writing

**A C H I E V I N G   A   S O C I A L   W O R K   D E G R E E**

This chapter will help you to develop the following capabilities, to the appropriate level, from the **Professional Capabilities Framework**:

* **Professionalism**
Describe the importance of professional behaviour.

* **Values and ethics**
Understand the profession's ethical principles and their relevance to practice.

* **Critical reflection and analysis**
Recognise and describe why evidence is important in social work practice.

* **Intervention and skills**
Demonstrate awareness of a range of frameworks to assess and plan intervention. Demonstrate basic ability to produce written documents relevant for practice.

It will also introduce you to the following standards as set out in the 2008 social work subject benchmark statement:

**5.5.2 Gathering information**

**5.5.4 Intervention and evaluation**

**6.6**  Students should engage in a broad range of activities, including ... a variety of forms of writing...

**6.9**  Assessment methods normally through ... essays, e-assessment and exams including an extended piece of written work normally in the final year.

## Introduction

You began by thinking about how to ask critical questions, moved through applying new strategies to your critical reading and now you will be able to use the skills of the last two chapters to look at how you begin to change the way you write. Essentially, critical writing is about convincing the reader that you have the knowledge upon which to make considered judgements. You should demonstrate your ability to use language in a convincing and persuasive way, present complex ideas clearly and simply, and be able to follow conventional English, syntax and grammar. In addition you will need to integrate coherence and logical flow into your arguments and ensure that the work resolves into an erudite conclusion based on evidence and rigorous argument.

By the end of this chapter you will be able to:

* understand how to write more critically;
* create sophisticated responses in writing;

- use several techniques to manage your writing;

- understand how to punctuate your work correctly;

- understand how to use creative writing techniques and how to avoid others.

# What is critical writing?

First it is important to say that critical writing must be underpinned by critical reading. It is not possible to write in a critical way if you are not able to detect critical arguments within your reading of the texts or in your understanding of knowledge. For example, you would not be able to write a critical essay about whether Islam is a religion or a political movement or possesses elements of both, if you were uninformed about the critical elements in such a debate.

So in critical writing you should intellectually be able to:

- put forward a central idea setting the scene and clarifying your assertions;

- show evidence that you are informed by a sense of creative discussion;

- demonstrate that you can appreciate and respond to the language and ideas of the debate;

- make decisions about the strengths and weaknesses of the arguments put forward within a debate;

- assess the coherence and flow of your own writing using data analysis and logical progression;

- make sure that the material you use is valid and trustworthy;

- demonstrate a clear and logical organisation of the debate.

Technically you should be able to:

- present a concise introductory paragraph that leads into your central idea;

- use English spelling, grammar, sentence construction, punctuation and paragraphs;

- conform to the required referencing system;

- express yourself clearly, directly and assertively/forcefully;

- use a new paragraph for each new idea and say how this relates to your central idea(s) – it is also useful to link the paragraph ideas together as this makes the work 'flow' more coherently;

- present a conclusion that summarises your debate(s)/argument(s) and shows how you have proved your central thesis/idea.

Critical elements will show how you are able to:

- select aspects that are open to question – assumption, opinion, conjecture;

- comment on the aspect(s) in a balanced way;

- select authoritative sources for researching the topic;

- question 'accepted' views;

- evaluate your arguments;

- position yourself within the debate in a critical way using self-analysis;

- consider your use of language – using erudite yet non-jargonistic terms.

# Writing as theatre

It may help you to think about how you might give directions to someone else in explaining what you want to write. It is vital that they really understand your meaning so that they can interpret it as correctly as possible for the 'audience'. Suppose you wanted them to understand what anti-discriminatory practice and anti-oppressive practice meant so that they could role-play it to the audience. First you would need to say that although these terms are often used together, they have different meanings. Then you would define the meanings and give examples of them to consolidate their understanding. Having understood this, they will be better able to pass this on to the audience.

---

**ACTIVITY 3.1**

**Defining terms**

*Write your own definitions of anti-oppressive and anti-discriminatory practice.*

*Have a go at this now and record your explanations in your learning log.*

---

## Comment

Did you go away and research the meaning of these two phrases? If you didn't, then do so now and check your definitions with the ones you find. You could try looking at Thompson's book *Anti-discriminatory Practice* (2006) and Dominelli's chapter 'Anti-oppressive practice in context' (2002).

So now you will be able to explain to the cast something like this.

Anti-discriminatory practice:

> *seeks to diminish and combat unfair and unequal treatment and to remove barriers that prevent people accessing services.*

Whereas anti-oppressive practice:

> *goes beyond this to challenge the structure of society and the use of power to maintain some groups in inferior positions.*

> (Open University course K113, Practice cards on http://openlearn.open.ac.uk/
> mod/resource/view.php?id=166551)

*57*

*Ok*, they say, *But can you expose what exactly it means in practice, give us an example?*

So you might say, *Well give me a few minutes!*

It is then you realise that to give an example you have to put these definitions into a context, in this case a practice setting so that others can understand how they work. In doing this you will be explaining to the reader that you also understand and are able to give credible explanations for what you describe. Even if you think the reader probably knows the answer, it is up to you to demonstrate clearly your own understanding rather than leave it to your reader to make assumptions about what you do and do not understand.

Now you have had a few minutes and the theatrical cast is waiting for your examples.

*Fine*, you say, *imagine you are arranging where to place a polling station for a local election. Usually the local library is used but it's up lots of steps and there is no lift. You know that older and disabled people and women with prams might be prevented from voting because of poor accessibility and so you present your justified response to not using the library to your local council. That is anti-discriminatory practice – often based on single issues but nevertheless a major contributory factor in the inclusion of certain people to enable them to exercise their rightful franchise.*

*Oh*, say the cast, *that's fine, we understand now, and off they go to create a sketch showing a scene at a local library and how impossible it is for some people to vote because of who they are.*

The cast then turns to you again. *Oh no*, they say, *but what about anti-oppressive practice, then, is that not the same?*

*No! Suppose the government uses statistics to show that older and disabled people and young mothers tend not to vote anyway so there is no point in shifting the traditional places for voting. There is a local expectation among the government's supporters that voting always takes place in the library. So you see the reason why these categories of voters don't vote is not because they are apathetic but because they can't access the library. The rule to continue to use the library is based on local and national power thinking about 'less valuable' people. It is possible that the government privately thinks that older or disabled people are less valuable. This view needs to be challenged and a fully accessible venue provided for voting.*

*Right, then, let's get Jane to create a mock-up of Number 10!*

In making yourself exemplify (explain through examples), you are demonstrating to the reader that you understand the debates. So seeing critical writing as theatre allows you to show how words carry meaning and performance roles, introduce assertion and questioning, give direction by confirming, evaluating, summarising and concluding through giving exemplars.

Of course, you have probably spotted that the audience in the first instance is the tutor who marks your work. Eventually, as you progress in your practice placement, you will be increasingly developing your arguments to support your perspectives and most of these will inevitably be expressed in reports advocating on behalf of service users, compiling case notes, commissioning services and providing references for others. So you see the ability to write critically is a major asset in your professional life.

# Using sophistication in your critical writing

The style of writing contained in the example above may not be suitable for academic writing but the ideas, being of a 'critical' nature, are suitable. The existing style is rather chatty and appropriate for the purpose of explaining what might go into a conversation. The idea of a 'conversation' is a useful one to keep in mind as you think about critical writing.

If we bring together the 'conversation' and the 'ideas' contained in this small passage it will allow us to fuse a demonstration of two or more 'speakers' with a variety of ideas. In doing so we demonstrate the capacity to juxtapose (set up opposing debates) the views of different protagonists (this just means people who join in the argument with different or opposing views) in explaining what themes are axiomatic (central) to the debate.

---

**ACTIVITY 3.2**

**Defining terms using academic/sophisticated writing**

*Let's suppose the question you were answering was:*

   Expose the purposes for using anti-discriminatory and anti-oppressive practice in social work.

*(By the way, this is a 'critical' question. How do you know? An answer is provided at the end of the chapter, p76.)*

*Make a plan for how you might structure your writing and put this in your learning log. You can use the examples given in the 'theatre'. Then go to the commentary section below and compare your responses. Try not to look at the responses first as this will limit your learning.*

---

## Comment

Look at these sentences from the text. It may help you to see how the use of sophisticated (not jargon) writing will improve your written work. The initial text is taken directly from the spoken 'theatre' example above with the variant of an academic style shown as (a).

1.  Suppose you wanted them to understand what anti-discriminatory practice and anti-oppressive practice meant so that they could role-play it to the audience. First you would need to say that although these terms are often used together, they have different meanings.

1(a) In order to explore why it is necessary to understand with clarity the purpose for using both anti-discriminatory and anti-oppressive practice in the social work profession, I primarily need to critically explore the meaning of the two terms.

2.  Then you would define the meanings and give examples of them to consolidate their understanding. (It is always useful to show your understanding before using a quote and then to exemplify in your practice after your quote.)

2(a) Essentially anti-discriminatory practice means that which is based on an understanding that certain people and groups are denied their rights to exercise generally accepted truths about living in society. They are discriminated against because of negative attitudes, how these affect policies and because of physical obstacles and barriers. Anti-discriminatory practice:

*seeks to diminish and combat unfair and unequal treatment and to remove barriers that prevent people accessing services.*

(Open University course K113 Practice cards on
http://openlearn.open.ac.uk/mod/resource/view.php?id=166551)

The implications for my own practice would be that I would need to be anticipatory in thinking about how service users access our provision; whether there are any design faults resulting in negative attitudes or barriers that have influenced how it is provided. I would also consult with service users and their carers to enhance our effectiveness.

Anti-oppressive practice recognises that through time certain groups have become more powerful and have used this power to make decisions that have treated those who are less powerful less favourably. These people have been oppressed because they are seen as less able, not as powerful, less important and often less intelligent. So anti-oppressive practice goes beyond anti-discriminatory practice

*to challenge the structure of society and the use of power to maintain some groups in inferior positions.*

(Open University course K113, Practice cards on
http://openlearn.open.ac.uk/mod/resource/view.php?id=166551)

What this means is that I would bring recognition to my practice that most of the people who access our service have not been given fair life chances and I need to try to redress that by advocating on their behalf and in joining organisations that challenge the hegemony (look this up in the glossary if you don't understand the meaning) of governmental and societal power mechanisms.

3. *Ok, they say, But can you expose what exactly it means in practice, give us an example?*

3(a) In order to exemplify these two concepts in practice I will look at the discourses around enfranchisement, in practice the right to vote. Low turnout, apathy and the use of a contentious 'first past the post' system have meant that election results have often elected candidates who have far fewer votes than the combined opposition. In order to increase the numbers of the voting public it would make good sense to recognise the inadequacies of the environment in which some polling stations are based. Governments and councils in office are disinclined to do this as they fear the increased turnout may disadvantage them in the next elections. Opposition councillors and ministers don't have the power to change the status quo.

4. *Fine, you say, imagine you are arranging where to place a polling station for a local election.*

4(a) In taking an anti-discriminatory stance, I shall examine the question of the voting environment. One clear barrier to access for older and disabled people and for young mothers/fathers with prams is the fact that many buildings used for polling are accessed only by steps. A simple solution would be to audit such provision out of the equation by making all venues physically accessible to everyone. Celebrating this as 'good practice' and raising it as a local issue would signal an acceptance that should encourage previously disenfranchised people to vote. In addition, the opening up of such anomalies demonstrates a willingness to deal with exclusive practice and has a humanising effect on society.

5. The cast then turns to you again. *Oh no*, they say, *but what about anti-oppressive practice, then, is that not the same?*

5(a) Alternatively, it is not only in the act of being denied one's rights because of some local difficulties that inequality exists. The broader business of how societies develop, are controlled and evolve is symptomatic of the impact of deeper discourses. To return to the issue of voting it is possible to see that individual concerns about access to polling stations are seen to be inconsequential and outweighed by the larger concerns of the war in Iraq, rising fuel charges and local use of greenfield sites. Politicians speak of apathy among the voting public, offer car rides to the polling station, send loud hailers around the constituency yet do not anticipate changing the way in which people can vote. They generally have no experience of such disadvantage and so cannot envisage the insurmountable difficulties the environmental barriers cause. This ignorance, coupled with a drive to use their power benignly in their own favour, has led to the development of a set of values and consequent upon them, practice, that has continued to use power to beget power.

6. Off they go to create a sketch showing a scene at a local library showing how impossible it is for some people to vote because of who they are.

*Right, then, let's get Jane to create a mock-up of Number 10!*

6(a) In exposing the arguments about using anti-discriminatory and anti-oppressive practice in social work I want to synthesise these into the purpose for doing so. My first premise is that people who are 'in need' should be helped back into society rather than estranged from it. This prevents the development of an underclass who become disassociated from societal norms. In order to do this, professional social workers must be able to effectively challenge both the macro and micro elements of society that seek to disadvantage certain individuals and groups. For example, the immigration laws (macro – oppressive) and the positioning of local services for sex workers (micro – discriminatory).

I previously alluded to the humanising effect that an exposed value of equity and fair treatment can have on society. It is inevitable that most of us will experience disability; some will struggle with young children and their accoutrements while using public services; and with luck most of us will reach older age. Along the way we may also experience periods of homelessness, debt or bereavement and succumb to mental ill health, drug or alcohol misuse. It is with sensitivity, support and advocacy that we will wish to be nurtured back to the equilibrium of our 'normal' lives. We can have hope that we will be seen as individuals rather than conditions or behaviours and that in the face of bureaucracies we will have allies in our caring professionals. So my second premise is that services should be appropriate to support me when I need them in that they will be quick to act, affordable, relevant and uphold my dignity and value.

My third premise is that a developed society has the capacity to support its members when they are in need and this capacity should not be diminished by government virement of money to support war, prop up failing banks for personal advancement or to bolster party popularity. Social work practitioners have a duty to challenge policy and practice, attitudes and behaviours that refute this notion.

Finally, I believe that in some situations the care-and-control debate becomes highly contentious. Social workers must use their power to act in the best interests of the individual and society. It is essential that social workers are able to dissect and reconstruct the purpose of their work, taking account of their legitimate power and of the shifting nature of the social work role. In removing an abused child, or refusing to admit an older person to institutional care at the family's request, social workers need to be accountable for their practice. Perceptions by the general public, the press and government are highly influential but social work is in a position to hold the middle ground between affirmation and vilification, and ultimately between order and unrest.

These four premises of inclusion, relevance, capacity and control form the four cornerstones of anti-discriminatory and anti-oppressive practice and their purpose within social work.

Of course, you would need to add a conclusion and some references from journals and texts, include some facts or statistics from research and write an introduction to the work. Essentially, this would be the bones of the assignment in response to the question.

However, in addition to this sophistication in your writing you will need to show that you are able to argue from differing perspectives. So you would also be looking at the impact that anti-discriminatory and anti-oppressive strategies can have other than the moral argument expressed above. You might include:

- the pressure this puts on you as a professional;

- having to justify your arguments when you may not be too clear about them;

- being seen as the 'contentious' one who always holds up decision-making;

- others feeling you are showing off because you are a university student;

- alienation from friends and family because you are too critical;

- being accused of being too PC ('politically correct', used as a derogatory term);

- the possibility of failing your placement because of your critical stance with your practice teacher (although 'critical' also means celebrating good practice);

- incurring the wrath of service users and carers because you tend to challenge the macro issues of the roots of oppression rather than acting on their immediate problem.

You can see how a critical essay will debate all these issues yet come to a balanced decision about theory and practice, so that theory is largely adhered to and practice is largely morally acceptable but that you become the architect of the process of synthesis between the two, your position changing as you become more competent.

# Towards critical writing – tips and tricks

### Stretching your ideas

Be creative and aspirational in how you think about what you write. Many students carry on writing just as they did before entering higher education and are disappointed when they find their grades are not improving. You have a responsibility to yourself to improve your writing skills. You will find that in Years Two and Three the criteria change and become more critical in nature. You may even find that your grades go down if you haven't tackled your critical writing in Year One.

A useful way to push yourself to be more critical is to challenge yourself to think about more and more areas to include in your debate while remaining focused. In Chapter 2 there was an example of a ripple diagram and a spider diagram. You can use these techniques with critical writing too, maybe using and adapting those created in your critical reading. Figure 3.1 is an example of how you might take each aspect of the critical reading example and build on it for critical writing. I have taken only one section in this spider diagram example. You can go on generating as wide a diagram as you have questions by creating other 'legs'.

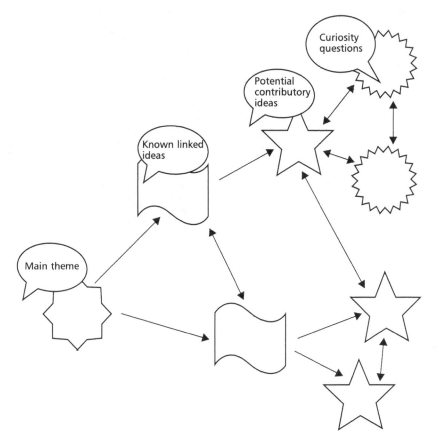

*Figure 3.1 Example of using a spider diagram*

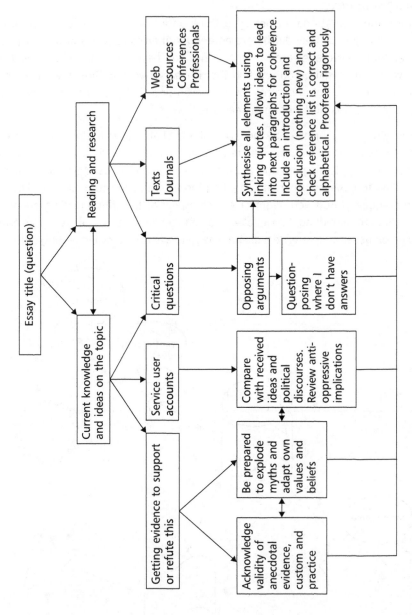

Figure 3.2 Example of using a flow-chart

Have a look at this example of a spider diagram about cycling:
www.camcycle.org.uk/newsletters/13/images/spiderlarge.gif

Here is a different spider
www.members.tripod.com/colla/mental/growth/spider.gif

When you are planning to write your next essay try using this technique.

You could also use a flowchart (Figure 3.2) but remember that this is a rather linear way of putting down your ideas and tends to lead you into a one-track argument rather than opening up all the possible debates. If you had headings leading from the main idea and then broadened each heading out into multiple ideas, this could work.

Take these diagrams and enlarge them if you want to use them in planning your critical writing.

# Moving from the apprentice to the master

Be critical of your own writing. Try writing a sentence or paragraph and then revisit it to do a rewrite – treat it as though it is just the first of many drafts.

Each time you redraft, use clearer sentences:

- take your chosen points a little deeper;

- evaluate your own arguments and see if they are convincing;

- look at the logical outcome and then see if there are any counter points;

- identify what aspects of the issue are open to question;

- analyse whether you think the issue has any validity;

- give clear evidence.

### Towards the master of critical trade

Here are examples of four types of answers to one question, moving from the apprentice to the master of critical trade. Let's suppose the question was:

*Explore the government's arguments about lone mother policy and give your own suggestions for change or continuity.*

| | |
|---|---|
| *Apprentice* | I know that government policy on lone mothers focuses on giving opportunities for access to work in order to lift them out of poverty. |
| *New employee* | In doing this the government promotes the view that lone mothers raise delinquent youths due to having no male disciplinarian. The view is that these women perpetuate a circle of dependency by being claimants and by raising children who underachieve and then find it difficult to obtain work, thus completing a cycle of dependency on the state. |

*Established employee*   I also know that there is no evidence to suggest that delinquency resides with lone-mother households. I have read that income maintenance for this group is inadequate. There is no access to affordable childcare and absent fathers fail to accept responsibility for their children. In addition, employers are inflexible, part-time work is poorly paid and insecure, and all this leads to lone mothers being stigmatised by social policy and media promulgation of blame.

*Master of critical trade*   A solution may be more appropriately targeted equality measures for working-class women, for those who can afford to pay would not fall under this discourse. Support for the creation of better community networks, advocacy and mediation services, and the sustainable support of income maintenance would challenge the role of women as the only carers. This could be actioned possibly through the appointment at Cabinet level of a Minister for Women. This would help to raise consciousness of current oppressive policy and practice.

Such a strategy would make connections between feminist theories of the rights of women, societal labelling about women as lone mothers, and the position of children and young people as our next parental generation. In this way the binary of middle-class male dominance would be challenged by an oppositional binary of working women and their rights to accessible and appropriate support as of right, and not because they are inadequate, weak and dependent members of society.

---

### ACTIVITY 3.3

*In your learning log identify which one of the above four categories most closely resembles where you think you currently fit. Then say where you would like to fit in one month's time and what you need to do to improve. Set yourself realistic tasks so that if you are at the 'apprentice' level you should aim for the 'new employee' level and then continue up the scale gradually.*

## Understanding how to use punctuation in your writing

This may seem simplistic but the use of punctuation is vital in critical writing. Beginning with the comma, look at this sentence.

*Woman without her man is nothing.*

How would you read it? Would you say that man is nothing without woman or that a woman without a man amounts to nothing? Two very different messages that could be presented with clarity with the addition of a comma.

*Woman, without her, man is nothing* 'Woman   without her   man is nothing.'

*Woman without her man, is nothing.* 'Woman without her man   is nothing.'

In the first sentence man is said to be nothing without a woman. In the second a woman without a man amounts to nothing. If it helps, try separating your sentences into phrases as above. This will show you where the commas should go. You can also try saying these phrases out loud. You will see that the tone and pitch of your voice changes. So using commas gives your written work a musical quality that in turn tells the reader how to interpret your sentences.

---

### ACTIVITY 3.4

**Using commas**

*Have a go at these.*

1. *He didn't marry her because he loved her.*
2. *The mother hit her head in the car with a fury.*
3. *The car arrived with the string band in a hurry.*
4. *The holiday was spoiled with certainty in the rain.*
5. *As he smacked her quickly she ran away.*

---

## Comment

Hopefully you will also have seen the humorous side of some of these. Check your answers with these at the end of the chapter.

If the comma gives music to your written work, then the apostrophe gives ownership.

*It's mine, said the girls' mother's husband.*

In this sentence the apostrophe in *it's* stands for a missing letter, in this case the second 'i' in 'it is'. The apostrophe after *girls'* shows that there was more than one girl. If it had been one girl then it would have been shown as *girl's*. Of course, in this case it does not stand for a missing letter but to show the possessive: it belongs to a pair of girls, or perhaps twins or triplets. Next the text indicates that there is only one mother – how do you know this? Yes, because of the position of the apostrophe. Fascinating isn't it! See that, it was an exclamation mark at the end of the sentence. This shows that I am being rather assertive, wanting you to agree with me. Perhaps also ironic or sardonic (not many people are actually fascinated by exclamation marks) and maybe a little hopeful that my point is well and strongly made. It also marks the end of a sentence, but don't use too many or you will be like the boy who cried wolf and devalue its power. No apostrophe in 'its' there because 'it is' would not be used.

---

ACTIVITY **3·5**

**Ownership and the disappearing letter**

*Have a go at these, are they correct or not?*

1. *It's a fabulous day today.*
2. *The babies' rattle's fell out of the pram.*
3. *My sock's are too small.*
4. *His father's answers' are untruthful.*
5. *The writers' points are well made.*

---

## Comment

The positioning of the apostrophe can influence readers in formal reports, so that in number 4 an incorrect positioning of the apostrophe as *fathers'* could indicate that the subject recognised more than one person as a father, and in number 5 we see that there are several writers making their points well.

Answers are provided at the end of the chapter.

Now let's (apostrophe is standing for a 'u' here) just think about the humble full stop. It's amazing how many people think there is a tax on them and so never use them. Consequently, the content of what they are trying to say just goes on and on, and eventually the points they are trying to make become more and more tied up together and the message they are trying to get over about what they understand about something or how they interpret it or any new concepts that have occurred to them just get buried in a field of words and a stream of consciousness that just never stops. (Breathe now.)

### Sentence construction

Here are seven things to do to improve your sentence construction; [see that, that's a semi-colon, designed to tell you that there is more to come].

1. Put the main point of the sentence at the beginning: (see that, that's a colon to deliver what the previous text has promised will be delivered) for example:

   *Due to the Community Care (Direct Payments) Act 1996 (C 30) many service users are purchasing their own services.*

Rather than:

   *Many service users are purchasing their own services because of the Community Care (Direct Payments) Act 1996 (C 30)*

2. Use the active rather than the passive voice:

   The case conference decided to review the situation in three months.

Rather than:

   *It was decided by the case conference that the situation should be reviewed in three months.*

3. Link phrases together sequentially rather than splitting the sentence:

   *Within an analysis of risk it is important to consider which theory is appropriate, what the implications will be and the impact of social constructionism on the outcome.*

Rather than:

> *Within an analysis of risk it is important to consider which theory is appropriate. The implications should also be thought about as should the social constructionism.*

4. Avoid putting several nouns together:

This is our strategy to engage our service users in participation with us.

Rather than:

> *This is our 'service user participation engagement strategy'.*

5. Avoid double negatives:

He wanted to have minimal contact with his children.

Rather than:

> *He didn't want to have no contact with his children.*

6. Use of pronouns. Make sure they are clearly related to the nouns:

> *Task-centred practice and cognitive behaviourism are two theories I have considered for use in my practice placement. These theories are the central theme of the assignment.*

Or *My practice placement is the central theme of the assignment.*

Rather than:

> *Task-centred practice and cognitive behaviourism are two theories I have considered for use in my practice placement. This is the central theme of the assignment.*

7. Short sentences are more easily understood than longer ones. Separate your ideas into clear and concise pieces of information:

> *Consequently the content of what they are trying to say just goes on and on. Eventually the points they are trying to make become more and more tied up together. The message they are trying to get over about what they understand about something or how they interpret it just gets buried. Any new concepts that have occurred to them are lost in a field of words and a stream of consciousness that just never stops.*

Rather than:

> *Consequently the content of what they are trying to say just goes on and on and eventually the points they are trying to make become more and more tied up together and the message they are trying to get over about what they understand about something or how they interpret it or any new concepts that have occurred to them just get buried in a field of words and a stream of consciousness that just never stops.*

# Tricks and tips – critical writing language

### The language of critical writing

Through the Manchester University website you will be able to access a 'word bank' that has been created to help students to construct a CV (www.manchester.ac.uk; go to the website search at the top of the page and enter 'word bank'). Here you will find a useful selection of alternatives to use in your critical writing.

In addition, think about using the following in your writing:

*Asinine* … foolish or stupid

*His stepfather made an asinine remark about the boy's biological father.*

*Assertive – assert* … stating or declaring in a forceful way.

*The researcher asserts that her heritage was a significant factor in the interpretation of the data.*

*Attestation – attest* … to make a true statement or promise.

*I can attest to the value of social work education.*

*Attenuate – attenuated* … weakened or less valuable

The powerful forces in the council chamber attenuated her position as a disabled person.

*Authenticate – authentic* … genuine and proved to be true.

*The charging policy was introduced as an authentic method of allowing more access to services.*

*Auspicious and auspices* … showing promise of success and the giving of help and support in order to succeed.

*The project began auspiciously under the auspices of the Macmillan Cancer Trust.*

*Axiomatic – axiom* … self-evident and not in need of proof, a generally accepted true statement.

*It is axiomatic that social work students must embrace the effects of social constructionism in order to successfully qualify.*

And these are only the 'A's!

You have a responsibility to educate yourself in the art of linguistic sophistication. This is not least because it makes your own writing more erudite (full of learning) but mostly because it gives you access to what you are reading. In one of her sketches, Victoria Wood, playing a 'groupie', stated that she had received a letter. When asked what it contained she was unable to say because in her words it was *full of spelling*. We don't seek to baffle the reader by using language that is inaccessible but should be able to express ourselves succinctly using language appropriate to our profession and level of our education.

Try using some of the above 'A's in your next assignment; and why not branch out into the 'B's and 'C's too?

### Using metaphor and simile to highlight learning

In sophisticated writing authors often use metaphor and simile to 'stand for' something else. In that way they can speed up the readers' understanding (and their own) by using a known concept to illuminate their understanding and learning.

Metaphor

Metaphor uses words or phrases to stand for or substitute for others.

For example: *You are my soul mate*; meaning I have a deep and well-established affinity with you that may be romantic, supportive or intellectual.

You can also use words that depict how something affects you, as the following examples show.

*Learning journey* and this can be shown visually by drawing or using a picture or photograph on which to hang the term. So you might show a picture of the ocean or a train, some mode of transport for your journey. You might use emotions to describe your journey; beginning with *apprehension* moving to *excitement* on to *anxiety, realisation, struggle, integration, consolidation, confidence* and finally *self-assurance*. The stage of your journey can also form part of the metaphor so you can introduce two islands in the ocean and you are moving from one (your current state of understanding) to the other (the position of understanding new knowledge and practice). What sort of a ship are you travelling in? Is it a yacht, a liner or a speedboat? Have you left the first island, how far across the sea are you, are you delayed by fog and when that clears do you find you need to navigate around rocks or icebergs? Do the driving rain and snow make your journey tedious and difficult, or is the sun shining with just a light breeze?

You might use your hobby as a metaphor for your learning. Hill climbing, mastering a new dance, football, learning to drive a car or baking. Or even take some household item such as a ladder, filing cabinet, wardrobe (what goes into it and why?). If you are interested in photography, then Tony Buzan's book *Use your head* shows how photographs can trigger ideas that link to metaphors for learning.

---

*ACTIVITY* **3.6**

**Using metaphor**

*Let's try to use a metaphor now. See what you can come up with for the following.*

*I would describe my learning on the social work course so far as' ...*

---

## Comment

You might have said something like the following.

A *juggernaut* of confusion. I seem to *dive out of the way of a huge lorry* only to be caught in the *path of a mini*. I plunge from one thing that I don't understand into another three that I can't get my head round. Everything is *coming at me so quickly* that I don't feel I have time to understand one thing before we *move on* and have to shift to others without having understood the first thing. This makes me feel anxious, a bit stupid and frustrated.

Sometimes I wonder if I am on the wrong *road*. I can't stop the rapid *speed* of learning about knowledge, theory, practice, values, ethics, and contexts but neither can I put the *brakes* on them. There is just too much *heavy traffic* for me to cope with.

You can see how the writer is using a traffic metaphor to describe her feelings of helplessness in the face of unfamiliar ideas, concepts and knowledge.

If you are feeling fine and comfortable about your progress, then you might have described your position using the metaphor of a spring garden. At first dormant and then slowly beginning to push above the soil, develop leaves and buds, then flowers and fruits, ultimately to seed and push energy into underground tubers, waiting for rebirth with each new idea.

Of course there are interesting positions to be had that are not so clear-cut but more of a mixture of emotions about progress and regression. This is especially true if you are finding that many of your preconceptions, taken-for-granted assumptions and common-sense notions of social work are all being exploded (there is another metaphor) and you are feeling stripped and empty. This is just a normal reaction to professionalisation and if you are experiencing it, then you are on the right road (there's that traffic metaphor again).

Can you think of any social work metaphors? Here are some examples.

*It was a* case study *of my life*. Stands for something replicating my life.

I was in supervision *trying to think about what went wrong*. Stands for a way of thinking, perhaps with a confidante, about why something went wrong and what to do.

We were on different planets! Stands for not understanding each other.

## Simile
Simile uses words that indicate a likeness to something.

For example: *He is like a father to her*. He is not actually her father but he behaves with beneficence like a father would do. (Assuming fathers are 'good'.)

*She went as white as a sheet/ghost*. The colour drained from her face.

*The audience were like putty in his hands*. He was able to manipulate the audience.

*It felt as though I had been hit with a restraining order*. I had been prevented from having access to someone.

Can you think of any similes that might be used in social work?

These work for me.

*He had a temper like a volcano*. His temper was sudden and fiery.

*She was as slippery as an eel*. She was difficult to get hold of.

*The children were as quiet as mice or as boisterous as puppies depending on who was looking after them*. The children were quieter when their mother was looking after them but more lively when in their father's care.

Of course you might think: why not just say it how it is? Yes, and you would be right, but it is important to recognise these expressions when used by others. In your critical writing you might want to use metaphor and simile to exemplify your critical thinking. In using such figures of speech we often communicate much more and in using critical thinking you will be questioning the messages contained in the writing and speech of others. You might question the phrase: *She went as white as a ghost*, when applied to a black service user. The phrase *She was as slippery as an eel* might imply a value judgement is being made about someone being slimy and untrustworthy. You should also be more aware of using these types of expression in your own writing and the hidden messages that they might communicate to the reader but that you had not realised or not intended.

Thinking of 'unintended meaning', I want to say a little about using cliché in your writing.

### A word of warning about cliché
The first thing to say is 'don't do it!' So what is a cliché? Generally defined, clichés are overused, worn-out, tacky remarks frequently issued by the guy or girl about town (that's a cliché) and often making you cringe.

Here are some from me:

*At the end of the day ...*

*Are you with me ...*

*That's easier said than done.*

*You can lead a horse to water but you can't make it drink.*

Don't think of any for social work but do recognise them when you see/hear them.

Here are some I have seen in student assignments.

*It shouldn't be allowed to happen.* (What and who is allowing it?)

*They should do something about it.* (Who and what is 'it' and why does something need to be done about 'it'?)

*Every cloud has a silver lining.* (A bit like a metaphor but what is deduced to be the cloud aspect and what is the silver lining I am looking for?)

*He didn't have a leg to stand on.* (That is also discriminatory language.)

*She turned the other cheek* (So is that!)

Not only is cliché boring to read, it doesn't give clarity of meaning but instead leaves the interpretation to the reader. It may seem obvious to the writer but you will lose marks if you put the burden of interpreting your meaning on to the reader.

Finally, when you have written your assignment, report, or whatever, you need to take a detailed look at it with a critical eye. Or get a trusted friend to do this for you, not some-one who will say only nice things about it. You can do the same for them too.

# Summarising and editing

These are crucial tools in refining your written work and whatever level of the stratosphere you achieve in your professional life your written work will always benefit from one or two stages of review.

Did you do précis at school? Well that is just what summary means. You take a longer piece of writing and, while retaining the meaning, reduce the length. You will find in your own work that you have expressed yourself rather long-windedly. Try to cut down the words and retain the content.

In editing your work you will read it with a view to correcting errors. Check that the facts are correct; do the expression, punctuation and sentence construction conform to written English: is the spelling OK? Is there anything you could condense; paragraph into sentence, sentence into phrase? Does anything need reorganising, come before or after something? Have you forgotten anything crucial or do you want to omit something that doesn't fit? You remember when you got up to make a drink, have you gone off at a tangent after that?

I have taken the themes from this chapter (and a few more) and put them into the following template to help you to review your work.

# A checklist for critical writing

| Intellectual abilities | Technical skills |
| --- | --- |
| Set the scene and clarify your assertions demonstrating a clear and logical organisation of the debate | Structure your work to include an introduction, paragraphs for each new idea and a conclusion |
| Show evidence that you are informed by a sense of creative discussion | Use grammatically correct English, spelling, sentence construction and punctuation |
| Demonstrate that you are responding to the language and ideas of the debate | Conform to the required referencing system |
| Make decisions about the strengths and weaknesses of the argument put forward in your debate | Express yourself clearly, directly and assertively |
| Assess the coherence and flow using data analysis and logical progression | Link paragraphs and say how each relates to your central theme |
| Make sure the material you use is valid and trustworthy | Present a conclusion that summarises your debate/arguments, and show how you have done what you set out to do in the introduction |

When you have done all this, read through again just to make sure that the changes you have made haven't disrupted the coherence and flow of your writing and the arguments it contained.

## CHAPTER SUMMARY

- Throughout this chapter I have given you some rather lengthy examples of critical writing in order to give you a sort of yardstick and to show you how this sort of writing differs from how you usually write. You should realise that developing critical writing in your academic life should be normal practice when you go into professional work. This means your placement too. There are many audiences for your work, from courts and case reviews to service users and their carers as they read their case files. The dispositions and skills discussed here are not about mystifying language but about using it with clarity, conciseness, without oppression and discrimination. Your representation of

*Continued*

**My haiku**
Writing with rigour,
from apprentice to master.
Clear and focused text.

**ACTIVITY 3.7**

*Now write your haiku for Chapter 3. How are you feeling about writing more critically?*

**FURTHER READING**

**Bowell, T and Kemp, G** (2005) *Critical thinking: a concise guide*. 2nd edition. Oxford: Routledge.

Chapter 5, 'The practice of argument reconstruction', will give you ideas on critical reading and is a useful text with many examples. Chapter 6, 'Issues in argument assessment', examines whether premises in an argument always lead to rational persuasion. So in being a critical reader you would seek to be persuaded about whether a statement is more or less likely to be true. This is a good skill in being able to assess evidence for the positions you hold and those you refute.

**Thompson, S and Thompson, N** (2008) *The critically reflective practitioner*. Basingstoke: Palgrave Macmillan.

Chapter 5, 'Recording and assessing reflection', usefully shows the differences between a variety of writing styles with some good exemplars of critical reflective writing. These are set within a social work context and are therefore realistic and directly applicable to your practice.

**Wallace, W and Wray, A** (2006) *Critical reading and writing for postgraduates*. London: Sage.

This text, although aimed at postgraduates, is very accessible and contains much of relevance to undergraduate study. It will be of particular benefit to those of you who intend continuing to postgraduate study or to post-qualifying studies once you have consolidated your practice after qualification. The book includes guidance on critical reading and critical writing, and will be of use in the previous chapter on developing critical reading too.

**USEFUL WEBSITES**

**www.kent.ac.uk/english/writingwebsite/writing/article3_p5.htm**

Two helpful pages on critical reading and writing with links to information.

**http://writing.upenn.edu/critical/help_tips.html**

This is a very practical website giving tips about how to write more critically using planning and argument analysis and guides you through writing for different purposes. Click on the links to find what you want.

# Answer to how you know it is a 'critical' question

This question doesn't ask you to define two concepts because that would only lead you to describe them in some way. It asks you to go further and use these two terms in social work, in other words say how you would practise them. You would create an argument making links between the two terms and their application in social work. The question doesn't give any value to the terms – whether they are good or not – so if you were a really critical thinker you could critique whether anti-oppressive or anti-discriminatory practice might also have negative effects for some people.

# Answers to the comma sentences

1.  He didn't marry her because he loved her.
    Was he married? He was married but didn't love his wife.
    A.  *He didn't marry her, because he loved her*. So maybe he didn't want to compromise her current position, wealth, etc.
    A.  *He didn't marry her because he loved her*. No, he married her for her money! No comma.

2.  The mother hit her head in the car with a fury.
    Whose head was hit? Did the car have a fury?
    A.  *The mother hit her head in the car, with a fury*. Mum bashed her head in the car because she was furious.
    A.  *The mother, hit her head in the car, with a fury*. Mum hit her sister's head while in the car and when she was furious.
    A.  *The mother hit her head in the car with a fury*. Mum caught her head on the fury in the car. (Supposing there is such a thing as a 'fury' – small hook-like protuberance.)

3.  The car arrived with a string band in a hurry.
    Was the band around the car or holding it together? Why was the string band in such a rush?
    A.  *The car arrived with a string band, in a hurry*. The car was in a hurry to divest itself of a large string quartet.
    A.  *The car arrived, with a string band in a hurry*. The string quartet was in a hurry to get to the concert hall on time.

4.  The holiday was spoiled with certainty in the rain.
    Was a little light rain responsible for spoiling the holiday? Was the forecast for torrential rain for 72 hours the cause of our spoilt holiday?
    A.  *The holiday was spoiled, with certainty in the rain*. The holiday was in a flood zone?
    A.  *The holiday was spoiled with certainty, in the rain*. We had taken only our bikinis with us so had nothing to wear in the rain.

5.  As he smacked her quickly she ran away.
    If he had smacked her slowly would she not have run away? Did she run away quickly having not liked being smacked?
    A.  *As he smacked her, quickly she ran away*. Who would stay around after being smacked?

A. *As he smacked her quickly, she ran away*. The quick and violent response shocked her and her reaction was to run away.

# Answers to the apostrophe exercise

1. It's a fabulous day today.
   Yes it is. The apostrophe stands for the missing 'i'.

2. The babies' rattle's fell out of the pram.
   This is more complicated. Here are several babies; each has a rattle so the first apostrophe is correct. The rattles that belong to them are just in the plural, adding an 's'. So no need for an apostrophe.

3. My sock's are too small.
   Although the socks are mine there is no need for an apostrophe because again there are two socks – so the 's' just shows the plural.

4. His father's answers' are untruthful.
   A possessive apostrophe in father's is correct but no need for one after answers.

5. The writers' points are well made.
   Correct, showing that I am commenting on several writers.

# Chapter 4

## Developing critical reasoning

ACHIEVING A SOCIAL WORK DEGREE

This chapter will help you to develop the following capabilities, to the appropriate level, from the **Professional Capabilities Framework:**

- **Professionalism**
Describe the role of the social worker.

- **Diversity**
Recognise the importance of diversity in human identity and experience, and the application of anti-discriminatory and anti-oppressive principles in social work practice.

- **Rights, justice and economic wellbeing**
Understand the principles of rights, justice and economic wellbeing, and their significance for social work practice.

- **Knowledge**
Demonstrate an initial understanding of the application of research, theory and knowledge from sociology, social policy, psychology, health and human growth and development to social work.

- **Critical reflection and analysis**
Understand the need to construct hypotheses in social work practice. Recognise and describe why evidence is important in social work practice.

- **Intervention and skills**
Demonstrate initial awareness of risk and safeguarding.

It will also introduce you to the following standards as set out in the 2008 social work subject benchmark statement:

4.4   Honours graduates in social work should therefore be equipped both to understand, and to work within, this context of contested debate about nature, scope and purpose, and be enabled to analyse, adapt to, manage and eventually to lead the processes of change.

4.7   The expectation that social workers will be able to ... think critically about complex social, legal, economic, political and cultural contexts in which social work practice is located ... and acquire and apply the habits of critical reflection, self-evaluation and consultation and make appropriate use of research in decision-making about practice and in the evaluation of outcomes.

5.1.3 Values and ethics

6.2   Conceptual understanding

## Introduction

The first three chapters of this book will have given you some skills with which to develop your criticality. These have been mainly within what we teachers call the affective domain.

That means they are strategies for how you might use models, forms, templates, descriptors and techniques for learning. This has involved you in thinking about these as you have worked through them but mainly you have been following guidelines either given by me or created by yourself.

I want to move you on now to a deeper level of work within the cognitive domain. This means that you are aiming to use creative and transformative thinking of your own. I will be able to give you some ideas but essentially I want you to create your own narratives on your learning. You can make the transformation from thinking about facts, opinions and assumptions to setting down your reasoning by using paragraphs and premises, and by being a persuasive protagonist.

By the end of this chapter you will be able to:

- analyse how to create and critique arguments, using evidence, in order to fully appreciate the nature of the service user environment;

- appreciate the contested nature of social work both in control and care, and risk and advocacy, and to employ a broader world-view of social work;

- be accountable in using your professional judgement;

- appreciate the attributes of professional social work along a continuum of technical rationalism and professional artistry.

# Human flourishing and transformative learning

Doing social work is about much more than just doing a job. While we can expect that most people would do their work with honesty and fairness, in social work we have the added dimensions of bringing our values and beliefs, fulfilling the Professional Capabilities Framework, working to the National Occupational Standards and meeting service users', carers' and employers' expectations of the profession. Additionally, we have what I call 'virtuous elements' to social work: those ways of thinking and practising that enable us to reason critically about the way we work; the impact of the work, and the dilemmas and tensions that it creates; the position our work holds in a world economy, in structural politics and social discourses; and the nature of our profession in working within a contested field of practice. These issues will be further discussed in Chapter 6 'Developing as a critical practitioner'. I mention these matters here because it is only through developing your ability in critical reasoning that you can become a critical practitioner. Becoming critical in your approach to the virtue contained in social work means that you always act as professionally as you can, using reasoning, premises to expose your arguments and having good evidence for your conclusions and potential impact of your actions. You do this regardless of whether you are under scrutiny and because to do otherwise would make you feel dissatisfied, uncomfortable and unprofessional. Being a social work student becomes a state of human flourishing for you in which you begin to take on the persona of social worker even from the first day of your course. The nature of this transformation really never ends, you are never able to say *I have arrived, I am now an expert social worker*, because experts have nothing more to learn. Incidentally, you cannot make these changes in your professional life without also making them in your personal life. You should expect to feel uncomfortable in certain situations and maybe uncertain how to deal with these. If you can work towards becoming more critical in your reasoning, you will have all the attributes to succeed. This transformative learning can cause you to feel unsettled but it is crucial in supporting you to work through the unforeseen situations that you are certain to encounter. Don't give up, you will move through it.

# Using premises and paragraphs

---

**ACTIVITY 4.1**

*Suppose you usually go to the pub with friends as part of your leisure activity. Since you have been on your social work course you notice that you have become uncomfortable about the jokes they tell. Often they are sexist but mainly they have a homophobic nature that you feel is demeaning and really not humorous at all. You really enjoy being with them otherwise and don't want to break friendship with them.*

*How might you deal with this situation? Write your responses in your learning log. Create a way of recording this that uses some of the techniques you used in the previous chapters, maybe a mind map or flowchart. You can then develop each of your reasons into a paragraph written in prose. (That just means written like this paragraph.) Use a new paragraph for each of your reasons.*

---

## Comment

Here are some possible responses.

(a) Make excuses to stop meeting with them. You feel unable to deal with it head-on and so decide to make some new friends, or just stay at home that night. You feel relieved that you don't have to put up with their behaviour any more and are happy with the decision even though it means you haven't stopped them from making these jokes.

(b) You talk the situation through separately with one of the group, asking what their views are about the tone of the jokes. You express your difficulties in dealing with them and say that you might have to stop meeting up if it continues. You feel rather nervous about mentioning the issue but explain a little about how you feel it is demeaning to people who just have different lifestyles.

(c) You continue to meet but each time you sense that the conversation is going the way of such jokes you absent yourself or try to divert the conversation on to another topic. This puts you under considerable stress as you feel you are policing the group.

(d) You decide to tackle the issue head-on with the group and rehearse what you are going to say and what their responses might be. You feel they might just say you are behaving 'like a student know-it-all' and are not sure how to deal with that.

(e) You are so outraged by their continued behaviour that you feel you have to say something even if that means that they won't want you to meet with them any more. You feel that you are so right in challenging them and that to not challenge would leave you feeling uncomfortable about your own collusion.

(f) You realise that you also used to enjoy these sessions of joke-telling but since learning about sexism and homophobia at university you have taken on some new beliefs and let previous ones go. You feel some of the group might be educated to see things differently but that others would not. They might stop telling the jokes when you are there.

Writing your responses down like this shows that you are able to reason in a way that examines the possible actions you might take, based on a rationale (reason why), and evaluation of the possible outcomes and impact on yourself and others. Just suppose your partner really liked you meeting your friends in the pub on that night because s/he had their friends round to the home on that night or used the quiet time to study. Your not going out would not only impact on you but also on those close to you.

If you write down your different responses as six different paragraphs (as I have done), you will see that you have created six different arguments and that each of these is based on one or more premises – statements or facts about something – so that in the first paragraph (a) the premises are as follows:

Premise 1. I am unable to confront the group about their sexist and homophobic jokes.

Premise 2. I would be relieved that I wouldn't have to put up with their behaviour.

The conclusion that follows is:

Conclusion: I will stop meeting with this group.

However, introducing a critical reasoning element you would have to say:

Premise 3: Their behaviour wouldn't change so I would be colluding with this continuation by not challenging it.

Premise 4: I would have to make a new set of friends.

So the conclusion may change to:

Conclusion: I need to devise some way of telling the group about my feelings so that I can remain comfortable about these meetings.

### ACTIVITY 4.2

*In your learning log, revisit your responses to Activity 4.1 and redefine them as premises and conclusions using critical reasoning.*

## Comment

Remember to use your cognitive skills and think through them in depth.

We have just looked at premises and paragraphs as a good way to begin. Now I want to look at two more 'P's, persuader and protagonist.

# Persuader and protagonist

These two ideas might at first seem mutually exclusive. Perhaps you think that persuasion is more about a kindly and gentle nurturing towards an agreement, while a protagonist would be more likely to challenge and take an adversarial stance (being an adversary against something or someone). Think about this idea by working through the following example.

---

### ACTIVITY 4.3

*A student social worker of South Asian descent, but born in England, was on placement in a maternity ward. She overheard two white midwives discussing some of the South Asian mothers-to-be, saying* They are like baby machines, just pushing out more children for the state to support. *While she did not feel able to challenge the midwives directly, she reported these comments to her line manager but no action was taken. She then reported the incident to her line manager's superior and was told that she was taking this too personally and she should examine her own sensitivity as a South Asian woman.*

*In this scenario the unprofessional behaviour was turned on to the student and as a black student she was subject to comments that would not have been made to a white student.*

*Certain assumptions were made about the mothers-to-be and these needed to be challenged, as did the attempt to persuade the student that she was at fault.*

*Write your initial feelings about this in your learning log. Do you agree with the comments of the line manager's superior or refute them? Why? What effect might this have on the student social worker?*

---

### Comment

How do you think this might have influenced the line manager's assessment of the student? How might the student's practice teacher respond to the situation?

Think about how, as a friend, you might have advised the student in acting as a persuader or a protagonist.

---

### ACTIVITY 4.4

*Using the example in Activity 4.3, imagine you advise the student to try to persuade her line manager and her superior that these comments were racist. Create premises and a conclusion resulting in a convincing argument. (It is worth noting this formula: Premises + Conclusion = Argument.)*

*Continued*

---

ACTIVITY **4.4** *Continued*

*You might choose to create a persuasive case or help the student to take on the role of protagonist. This will depend on whether you think her superiors are ignorant of the cause and effects of racism or they are actively racist.*

*Don't lose this material; keep it in your learning log.*

## Comment

Did you find that you were actually making the same argument in the end but the way in which you framed your premises and arguments were rather different?

In the case of persuasion you were probably expecting that the hospital staff were ignorant and that their reactions could be changed through some staff development. In the second case, taking on these issues as a protagonist you were probably thinking that the midwives' statements necessitated action being taken through a complaints procedure, possibly checking out what action was laid down in the hospital procedure against any staff in this position. Although the two stages would both result in some action for change, the first would allow for a nurturing process while the second would go straight to a potential disciplinary process. You might take this example further by taking the matter to the hospital senior management board and ultimately to the press and media, your position here being sensitive to the fact that you are a student and you don't want this to put your placement in jeopardy. Of course, the same would apply when you are an employee and you may fear losing your job.

In applying this example to the activity outcome, you can see that critical reasoning is a sequential process that pushes the boundaries of our thoughts and actions towards being able to realise all the possible outcomes of our actions through being full of thought. In social work that 'thought-fullness' is embedded in people's human rights, power and anti-discriminatory practice even where they are not our service users or carers, as in this case. Read the following account about a student social worker's weekend visit to a restaurant.

ACTIVITY **4.5**

*An anecdotal example of this expansion of anti-discriminatory practice was from a student where she and a friend visited a restaurant only to find that a blind man was refused entrance because the owner stated that the man's guide dog was a health hazard. The student tried to persuade the owner but he stood his ground, saying that the dog might prevent people from escaping if there were to be a fire. No doubt everyone would go out of her or his way to fall over the dog and thus be prevented from leaving before being overcome by smoke! (Irony is often a good way make the ridiculous apparent!) The student went to each diner, asking them if they would object to the man and his dog, bearing in mind the owner's reasoning. None did. The owner still refused to allow the blind man into the restaurant and so the student left and invited other diners to do so too. Some did.*

## Comment

This student demonstrated the qualities of a virtuous social worker in that she was uncomfortable when the man was refused entry and took the owner to task, eventually leaving the premises and taking other diners with her, causing the owner to lose business. She knew she was within the law – Disability Discrimination Act 1996 – and just imagine if she had colluded with the decision and remained to have her meal. Do you think she would have enjoyed it – would you?

# Technical rationalism and professional artistry

McCormack and Titchen (2006) have applied the work of Schön in their approach to critical creativity. Schön presents an argument about two opposite dispositions and I have applied these to current social work (and other professional) practice. At one end of a continuum is a technical rationalist approach (TR) that deals with the 'facts' in social work activity through systems of accountability, form-filling, economic rationality (the most effective and least costly solutions), efficiency and performance measurement that is geared to continuous improvement. At the other end is the professional artistry approach (PA) that deals in intuitive, creative, lateral thinking developed through experience and promoted mainly through critical reflective thinking and understanding. See Figure 4.1.

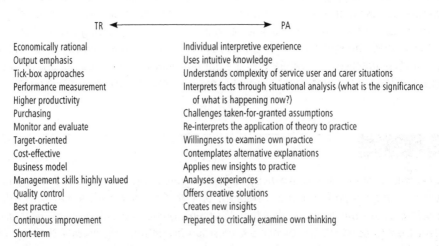

Figure 4.1 *Continuum of technical rationalism (TR) and professional artistry (PA)*

Look back to Activity 4.3 and the scenario of the maternity ward. I want you to think about how you could develop both TR and PA in looking at this situation.

ACTIVITY **4.6**

*All you have to do is to put in 'TR' or 'PA' – easy isn't it?*

*Think about which end of the continuum these statements would tend to belong.*

|   |   | TR or PA? |
|---|---|---|
| (a) | The ward completes records of complaints made | _____ |
| (b) | There is more willingness to reflect on practice | _____ |
| (c) | A more open culture allows for the reinterpretation of current practice | _____ |
| (d) | The emphasis is on continuing improvements in meeting targets | _____ |
| (e) | Creative solutions are encouraged | _____ |
| (f) | The assessment records consider only the medical model | _____ |
| (g) | Facts are preferred above intuition and knowledge experience | _____ |
| (h) | Staff are encouraged to use reflective practice | _____ |
| (i) | The Race Relations Act is formally implemented | _____ |
| (j) | Practitioner skills are highly valued | _____ |
| (k) | Standard output targets are implemented | _____ |
| (l) | Case reviews include the views of all stakeholders | _____ |
| (m) | A standard monetary amount is notionally allocated to each service user | _____ |
| (n) | Situations are focused around significant events | _____ |
| (o) | Thinking practices are challenged | _____ |

## Comment

In most bureaucratic organisations systems grow to cope with complexity so that the larger the organisation is and the longer it exists, the more regulation through form-filling activities there will be. The hierarchy becomes a tall structure where accountability of the lower levels is demonstrated by a paper trail for those at the top. This tends to lead to a technical rationalism often smothering creativity. Generally in more organic organisations the flat management structures lead to a sharing of experience in a way that values the essence of that experience. The nature of it is open to debate and analysis that lends itself more to creativity, challenge and growth. However, those organic organisations commissioned to provide services for the bureaucracies are seduced into their systems of regulation and accountability.

Check the suggested responses to the questions at the end of the chapter.

I want you now to think about justifying your responses to Activity 4.6.

ACTIVITY **4.7**

*In your learning log take each of your responses and justify why you responded as you did using critical reasoning. For example, in (a) you might have said that the answer was TR because records signify accountability and by giving a paper-trail of who made a complaint about what or whom, then it is possible to build up a dossier of evidence upon what action*

*Continued*

ACTIVITY 4.7 *Continued*

*can be taken. You could then go on to say that it is also possible to keep such records but never to do anything with them. So the records of complaint may be kept to comply with procedures but if no process of implementation is clear, then no action will result. So the system falls in on itself and apathy results as staff know that they will be immune to any action being taken through the disciplinary process due to lack of clear process.*

## Comment

When you present two (or more) alternatives like this you show that you understand that in the caring professions situations are rarely black or white but more nuances or shades of grey. Taylor and White (2006) encapsulate this whole area of uncertainty as they refer to the position of 'respectful uncertainty' that should be occupied by contemporary social workers, rather than the attempts of the profession to make certain the uncertain. Normally situations possess both TR and PA and fall somewhere along that continuum but rarely at the polemic extremes. This is one of the characteristics of critical reasoning – that you find yourself able to argue both for and against something at the same time. You become able to see the nuances of practice; like removing a child through care proceedings even though they are very loved by their parents, or allowing a looked-after child to return home where the living conditions are not materially suitable. In both cases you will need to defend your actions through critical reasoning, taking account of risk, power and anti-oppressive practice.

# Identifying assumptions, bias and hidden agendas

The professional artist will use a skilful approach in excavating (digging out) and scaffolding (building up) their critical reasoning in order to create convincing and persuasive arguments, and to act as a protagonist in challenging weak or discriminatory arguments.

The following example shows how assumptions, bias and hidden agendas might be contained in a report about a service user.

ACTIVITY 4.8

*Mrs F is an overweight woman who is a heavy smoker. There were empty beer cans in an overflowing refuse bin and the children's clothes were dirty. There was little evidence of toys for the children to play with although there was a new television in the sitting room. I suggested that Mrs F might like to join a local women's slimming group but she declined even though I offered to go with her.*

*Answer this question in your learning log:*

*What assumptions is the writer making here and what is the likely impact of these?*

# Comment

You might ask the following questions for clarification:

What is the definition of 'overweight'?

What is the impact of her smoking on the children?

Whose beer cans are they and when was the refuse last emptied?

Is there access to a working washing machine?

Did you spot any bias?

Toys can be made from household objects; they don't need to be expensive plastic purchases. The creation of a toy economy stems from a Western ideology that children need more and better quantities of plastic in order to keep up with their peers – an ideology created by toy producers and the media.

The new television may have been a gift or prize in a competition. If poorer parents, of necessity, spend most of their time in the home, then access to information and entertainment through a television could be seen as vital.

Were there any hidden agendas?

What constitutes a 'heavy smoker'? Although we know it is not healthy for children to be in smoky environments, Mrs F may smoke only outside the back door. There is an implication in the report that she should not smoke at all.

There is an implication that the reporter thinks toys should be purchased before a new television.

The message given by reference to attending a slimming club is that the social worker clearly thinks Mrs F is overweight. Offering to go with her seems to imply surveillance rather than support. Low-income diet is often indicative of weight gain as cheaper foodstuffs contain more quick energy.

Instead, think about how the following report on the same visit is different.

---

ACTIVITY **4.9**

*Mrs F was attempting to manage a meagre family budget for her large family. She did state that she felt under considerable stress and used cigarettes to help alleviate this. When I expressed concern about any danger that this might create for the children she assured me that she knew the risks and always smoked in the back yard.*

*There was evidence of empty beer cans in the kitchen but these did not appear to be excessive. I suggested that perhaps these could be put in a place where the children were not likely to have access to them. Mrs F said that her refuse bin was full because she had forgotten to put it out in time for the last collection. I had noticed over the last few visits*

*Continued*

*that the children seemed to be wearing dirty clothes. I carefully mentioned this to Mrs F and asked if she needed any help with washing facilities. She mentioned that although her machine had broken she managed so far to use the bath water to wash with. There was little evidence of toys for the children to play with and so I made a note to find out if I could put her name down for the charitable toy gifts at Christmas. I didn't want to raise her expectations nor did I want to offend her if she was opposed to accepting 'charity' so I thought it better to get correct information before asking her if I could put her name down. I asked her if she enjoyed her new television and she remarked that it was a real lifesaver as she was tied in with the children. I asked Mrs F if she knew that the local community centre had started some women's groups and asked if she would like me to find some information for her. As they had a crèche, it may be possible for her to make some local contacts.*

## Comment

Activity 4.9 shows how, using critical reasoning, the social worker was able to dig down to think of some reasons why Mrs F might be in her current situation; and then to build up a constructive approach to supporting her. We can also call this use of critical reasoning being 'non-judgemental'. This doesn't mean we don't make judgements but that we use anti-discriminatory and anti-oppressive thinking in making them.

The report in Activity 4.9 exposes the worker's use of empathy; that they were able to put themselves into the situation and begin to think as Mrs F might have done. The worker uses reflexive thinking in anticipating what Mrs F's reaction might be to being offered toys at Christmas and makes a note to find out if it were to be a possibility before returning to discuss Mrs F's feeling about this at a later date. Instead of broaching the subject of slimming in an authoritarian way, the worker offers Mrs F the opportunity to find out what is on offer at her local community centre after her comment about feeling 'tied in' with the children. The worker is able to use self-criticism 'in the moment' by anticipating what impact the intervention might have. This ability to reason critically by using empathy, self-monitoring and an anti-oppressive approach ensures social workers are able to present authenticity with clarity while considering the wider aspects of social justice. In terms of a theoretical basis for this meeting, the social worker should be applying one of the feminist approaches to the position of women who, being the lone parent, are often blamed for the situation they find themselves in.

Cottrell (2005) helps us with certain words that we can use to denote our critical reasoning:

*To signal the opening of an argument we could use, firstly; to begin with; initially; at the outset.*

*Following this we might want to introduce more themes; similarly; equally; likewise; in the same way. Or different themes; in addition; besides; also; as well as.*

*To strengthen our argument; furthermore; moreover; indeed; what is more.*

*To demonstrate that we hold a balanced view we could include the alternative points; alternatively; others argue that; it could be argued that.*

*To rebut others' arguments in order to strengthen our own; however; on the other hand; nonetheless; notwithstanding this.*

*To contradict and contrast; conversely; by contrast; although; exceptionally.*

*To express results and consequences; as a result; consequently; because of this; hence; thus.*

*By way of concluding; in conclusion; as a result; therefore.*

Using these words indicates to the reader that you are processing your critical reasoning skills and giving evidence for your thoughts and decisions.

---

### ACTIVITY 4.10

*Using the example of Mrs F and your critical reasoning, create a report that might have been used by this social worker to argue for the children to remain in the home environment rather than be received into the care of the local authority. Use some of Stella Cottrell's indicator words. Put this in your learning log.*

---

## Comment

You might have begun like this:

*Initially I will outline the situation Mrs F is facing at present with regard to the proposal to monitor her care of the children pending possible reception into care of the two youngest children. Similarly I will include reports from her health visitor and schoolteacher. In addition I will represent the views of her sister and older son who propose to offer their support to Mrs F. Furthermore, I shall offer the views of the two younger children through facilities offered by the local Family Support Service and alternatively conclusions reached by the educational psychologist following an assessment of these two children. However, in my observations there appears to be a strong maternal–child bond between Mrs F and her six children while there remain some fundamental areas in which behaviour change must be achieved if the children are to remain in her care. Although Mrs F agrees this to be the case there has been virtually no improvement since we began our involvement with her over three years ago. This suggests that new strategies need to be employed and in conclusion I would want to suggest that this meeting makes firm proposals after hearing the evidence presented today.*

The report would then go on to detail the information in the reports and to give your reasons for arguing that the children should stay in Mrs F's care.

# Critiquing others

Of course you are not only using critical reasoning in your own writing and debating but also in your critique of others.

Cottrell identifies these skills as involving:

> *identifying their reasons and conclusions; analysing how they select, combine and order reasons to construct a line of reasoning; evaluating whether their reasons support the conclusion they draw; evaluating whether their reasons are well-founded, based on good evidence; identifying flaws in their reasoning.*

> (Cottrell, 2005, p3)

Additionally, Cottrell goes on to include a definition given by Saskatchewan Education Department relating to critical reasoning and stating that

> *critical reasoning is about the application of intelligences: visual, musical, spacial, interpersonal, bodily, logical and linguistic. So that the skills of classifying, anticipating, comparing, identifying, informing, summarising and observing are deepened in their critical elements by a knowledge of – morality, needs and feelings of others, one's own discipline, self critique and practice knowledge.*

What a lively definition. It really spurs you into action! Overlay on to this the dispositions of – persistence, sensitivity, curiosity, creativity, commitment to change and growth, open-mindedness, honesty, objective/subjective understandings and lateral thinking, and you have the very essence of a critical reasoning practitioner.

So in Mrs F's example you might expand your analysis of her situation to the globalisation of wealth, the social construction of childhood and a feminist analysis of women's emancipation (or not). These issues are fundamental to how she is situated in the world but often remain unexposed and taken for granted as the norm.

# Thinking about thinking

I began this chapter by talking about critical reasoning being in the cognitive domain. Now I want to move you on to understand that meta-cognition refers to how we are able to think about how we, and others, think – thinking about thinking. In doing this you will be thinking about the reasoning, motives and arguments of others. You will have the ability to see all sides of the question and analyse its strengths and weaknesses. A good technique to help you to develop this is to depersonalise when you are reading or debating. Stand back from the personalities, however persuasive or combative they are, and focus on the content of what is being said. Try to expose the flaws, prejudices, bias and weaknesses while preparing to examine those things in yourself too. Be prepared to change your own stance in the light of the persuasive arguments of others. Be well organised and methodical in your attempts to reach learning goals. Perhaps you could try to develop your meta-cognition by offering a critique of a television programme or newspaper article. The Jeremy Kyle show should give you considerable material for this. Examine your initial thoughts and open up your own prejudices, and seek problem-solving that is ethical and imaginative, original and contemplative (allows you to contemplate potential implications of your thinking).

---

### CHAPTER SUMMARY

- This chapter has shown you that critical reasoning is borne of knowledge, meta-cognition and humility. By this I mean that you need to find a way of substituting a knee-jerk response for a more open self-critique while at the same time framing arguments to challenge the weaknesses in the arguments of others. Good critical reasoning enables the bringing together of incisive questioning, focused reading and clear writing. It is a developmental activity, just like riding a bicycle; once achieved you want to do it all the time and it is impossible to unlearn how to do it. There are rarely standardised 'right' answers to reasoning critically but answers that reflect the diversity, creativity, cultural groundedness and intellectual suppleness of human flourishing. This chapter has introduced you to techniques, language and strategies that will help you to develop your critical reasoning skills. You should understand how to apply critical reasoning to your knowledge, ways of thinking and to how you might challenge the thinking of others. In doing this you will be able to expose bias and assumptions, using evidence, and eradicate fallacy and question truth within a contested area of professional life.
- This is a great time then to move into Chapter 5, 'Developing a critical approach using multiple intelligences'. In this chapter there is an expectation that you will bring to bear all the skills and dispositions you have acquired through working with the examples and activities in the preceding four chapters.

**My haiku**
Reasoning, for me
the deep life-blood of practice.
Never-ending thoughts

---

### ACTIVITY *4.11*

*Try writing your 'reasoning' haiku in your learning log now. This is quite a difficult one to write but it is OK to say that in the haiku if that is how you feel.*

---

**FURTHER READING**

Taylor, C and White, S (2006) Knowledge and reasoning in social work: Educating for humane judgement. *British Journal of Social Work*, 36 (6), pp 937–54.
An invaluable text that is quite easy to understand and apply.

Thompson, A (1996) *Critical reasoning: A practical introduction*. London: Routledge. Some good examples with lengthy explanations that at times seem rather laborious. However the examples will help you to see the point straightaway even though they are not social-work related.

**USEFUL WEBSITES**

**www.questia.com**
enter 'moral reasoning – Anne Thomson' in the search box and then click on *Critical Reasoning in Ethics: A Practical Introduction,* then click Chapter 1. You can search through her book online for pithy definitions and examples providing useful ideas.

# Suggested responses to the TR/PA Quiz

| | TR or PA? |
|---|:---:|
| (a) The ward completes records of complaints made | TR |
| (b) There is more willingness to reflect on practice | PA |
| (c) A more open culture allows for the reinterpretation of current practice | PA |
| (d) The emphasis is on continuing improvements in meeting targets | TR |
| (e) Creative solutions are encouraged | PA |
| (f) The assessment records consider only the medical model | TR |
| (g) Facts are preferred above intuition and knowledge experience | TR |
| (h) Staff are encouraged to use reflective practice | PA |
| (i) The Race Relations Act is formally implemented | TR |
| (j) Practitioner skills are highly valued | PA |
| (k) Standard output targets are implemented | TR |
| (l) Case reviews include the views of all stakeholders | PA |
| (m) A standard monetary amount is notionally allocated to each service user | TR |
| (n) Situations are focused around significant events | PA |
| (o) Thinking practices are challenged | PA |

# Chapter 5

## Developing a critical approach using multiple intelligences

## Introduction

Chapter 4 looked at critical reasoning. How we reason depends upon our knowledge, skills, values and beliefs, the use of a multiplicity of complex interactions depending on our attributes and how we have experienced the world so far. Reasoning involves our emotional engagement within problem-solving situations. In the early 1980s the psychologist Howard

Gardner saw that the human brain can apply many 'intelligences' in addition to areas of logic (mathematics) and verbal (linguistic) abilities that are usually subject to testing to indicate IQ (Intelligence Quotient) levels. He called this his theory of Multiple Intelligences (MI).

Following this in the 1990s Daniel Goleman, a psychologist, working with an American Business Studies Professor, was keen to respond to queries as to why high-achieving graduates did not necessarily make the best employees, whereas those with lower grades but who possessed good intuition, could read difficult situations and respond with a 'can-do' approach. The latter group was group-orientated yet could lead and pursue individual goals and were seen by their employers to be the better workers. He went on to develop his ideas of Emotional Intelligence (EI).

The final strand of this triumvirate (threesome) of new thinking are the ideas expressed in texts by David L. Cooperrider and Diana Whitney (2005). Stemming from the Case Western Reserve University School of Management in the USA, and around 1985, thinking had begun to see the area of Change Management as being more about using a strengths-based approach than focusing on problem solving and gap-filling. This became known as Appreciative Inquiry (AI), a system of working that used positivity to build strengths in organisations and systems.

This chapter will open up these ideas and encourage you to see both the possibility of their application to social work and to create your own synthesis of their application to your practice. You will then be able to take your learning into Chapter 6 and your development as a Critical Practitioner. A synthesis of Chapters 4, 5 and 6 will take you on a journey of personal development that will support your learning in your social work degree, through completing a Masters programme and into your Assessed and Supported Year in Employment (ASYE).

Goleman analysed the roots of these skills using the emotional content inherent in their application and has given us the Emotional Intelligence (EI) framework for the development of critical practice as exemplified in Chapter 6 of this book.

By the end of this chapter you will be able to:

- identify the constituents of MI, EI and AI in your thinking;

- apply these terms in practice;

- recognise the power to act in organisational contexts;

- appreciate the relevance of MI, EI and AI to professional leadership.

# What are multiple intelligences?

Increasingly, the practice of social work is being impacted upon by ideas of globalisation, austerity, new managerial and theoretical approaches, accountability and the erosion of values and legal requirements (Kline and Preston-Shoot, 2012, p20). Kline and Preston-Shoot also speak of the contrast between the purported morality of health and social care professionals while at the same time having to deal with the complexity, oppositional discourses of actual practice, and theory and the pressure of real-time practice. This indicates that there is more to social work practice than knowing and applying the knowledge, skills and theory. Consequently, this chapter will explore how our emotions and appreciation of the complex situations in which we work can infuse and envelop practice so that we consider how we may develop a 'Multiple Intellectual Approach'. These ideas are founded in Howard Gardner's (1993, 1999) definition of nine areas of Multiple Intelligences (MI) and the premise that intelligence is not limited only to the usually tested abilities in verbal-linguistic and logical-mathematical areas. Along with these, Gardner also included intelligences in musical, spatial, bodily-kinaesthetic, intrapersonal, interpersonal, natural-istic and existential intelligence. Although it is clear to see that intra- and inter-personal intelligence are directly appropriate to social work, a theory of MI would demonstrate how all these domains are relevant. In Table 5.1 I attempt to relate each of Gardner's domains with descriptors for social work.

*Table 5.1 Gardner's MI domains in relation to social work practice*

| Gardner's MI domain | Descriptor and social work application |
| --- | --- |
| Verbal-linguistic | the ability to use words appropriately and effectively depending on audience and purpose<br>e.g. using reasoning, abstractions, express oneself simply, use persuasive argument, clear writing, critical reading in research, reports and service user records. |
| Logical-mathematical | the ability to see logical patterns and relationships<br>e.g. the synthesis of services to execute economically rational savings while maintaining or improving services. Use action research to justify new or jettison old provision. |
| Musical | the ability to recognise rhythmic and tonal patterns of communication and possess a sensitivity to environmental sounds<br>e.g. using sensory acuity to anticipate service user and colleague mood/attitudes, |
| Spatial | the ability to perceive the visual-spatial world accurately<br>e.g. to recognise potential risks in the environment to service users/colleagues/self and to appreciate the needs of others for privacy, solitude or companionship. |
| Bodily kinaesthetic | the ability to use the body to express emotion<br>e.g. to be aware of overt and covert messages portrayed in working with others and to use or hide these in oneself while recognising clues in others and responding appropriately to these. This area is particularly important in the area of risk and protection. |
| Intra-personal | the ability to act adaptively to self-knowledge<br>e.g. to develop a capacity for self-discipline, self-esteem and critical reflection in the giving and receiving of supervision and in examining one's values, beliefs, temperament, motivations and desires. |
| Inter-personal | the ability to work co-operatively, communicate through a repertoire of verbal and non-verbal and visual presentational methods<br>e.g. to be sensitive to, anticipate and access the best ways in which to communicate with others in order to demonstrate persuasive argument, appropriate ways to challenge, transparency and professional behaviour and to work effectively in contentious, complex and highly-charged situations. |
| Naturalistic | the ability to master taxonomy and show sensitivity to features of the natural world and demonstrate an understanding of different species<br>e.g. to be appreciative of the stages of the life cycle, the juxtaposing of the nature/nurture debate, an appreciation and a capacity to act on the importance of human value for the oppressed, the poor and the outcast in society. |
| Existential | the ability to pose questions and realise the ultimate realities of human existence in a complex world<br>e.g. to hold an appreciation of the nature of a multiplicity of personal existences and their spirituality and to know when/how to work with change and continuity with service users, colleagues, self and within agencies and policy makers. |

Adapted by the author from Gardner (1998)

---

**ACTIVITY 5.1**

**Mary's case study and MI**

Have a look at the case summary below and, taking Gardner's MIs as applied to social work as guidance, write a critical commentary in your learning log showing how links can be made between these domains and the case example.

Mary is a 73-year-old single white woman who has recently been accommodated in a small flat from a series of residential psychiatric provisions where she has lived since she was 18. Upon taking her case you have obtained her case notes from previous years (these are in paper form) and discovered that she gave birth to two children while in care. One was shortly after she entered care and the other was five years later while still in care. She believes both children died at birth. You read that both newborns were healthy and were put for adoption due to the fact that Mary was not considered a capable or fit mother.

---

## Comment

You might like to begin your examination by selecting both intra- and inter-personal domains first. This will encourage you to select the areas you need to think about (intra-personal), for example:

What are my personal views on Mary's history and the discrimination she may have encountered in being an unmarried mother?

Does the birth of a second child while in care mean that she may have been sexually abused/exploited?

How might I assess whether to encourage Mary to gain access to her files and how would I be able to support her with this knowledge?

What skills would I need to use in either protecting or exposing Mary to this knowledge (inter-personal), for example:

What communication skills would I use in order to anticipate Mary's reaction? She may have suspected the babies were alive, or have insufficiently grieved for them.

What probing questions might I use, or anticipate from Mary. For example, about what it might be like to have a family or grandchildren?

In raising Mary's awareness about the existence of information about her and her legal right to see this, what other professionals might you consider appropriate to involve with Mary's permission?

Continue to work through the domains of MI in this way and then consider what clusters may go together. For example, the inter-personal, bodily-kinaesthetic and spatial domains seem to fit. Whereas logical-mathematical seems to sit alone except where you consider the application for systems and resourcing to support Mary. So the domains can be used in tandem or in sequence as relevant.

University Centre Library
The Hub at Blackburn College

**Customer ID: ******50**

Title: Critical learning for social work students
(Second edition.). [Transforming social work
practice; Reflective reader]
ID: BB60909
**Due: Tue, 19 Nov 2019**

Total items: 1
22/10/2019 12:52

Please retain this receipt for your records
Contact Tel. 01254 292165

We will use this case study again when exploring two further areas of 'intelligence', namely those of Emotional Intelligence (EI) and Appreciative Inquiry (AI).

# Emotional Intelligence (EI)

EI remains a contested concept within the world of psychology where scientific critique (Eysenck, 2000) claims that it makes unsubstantiated claims about skills and aptitudes, supposing them to be intelligences. Locke (2005) similarly claims that what is defined as emotional intelligence by Goleman (1998) is in fact the use of intelligence as a skill applied to one area of life, namely the emotions. Psychologists working in the positivist paradigm have historically deconstructed intelligence to include the emotional state along with abilities, achievements, skills, habits, attitudes, values and personality traits. They have therefore categorised the 'emotional' as merely one of a series of components of intelligence itself rather than as a separate entity. They find it inappropriate to define 'emotional intelligence' as in any way distinct from, say, 'achievement intelligence' or 'skills intelligence' and so forth.

However, while it appears that positivist scientific research has shown a lack of validity and reliability in predicting EI, the skills sets that have been identified through scientific rigour do prove useful to social work. It is in the recognition of these and therefore the potential for personal development that I have included them as part of the MI construct.

Increasingly in the early 1990s researchers began to interpret the use of EI in the workplace (Salovey and Mayer, 1990) as a social intelligence used to guide thinking and action in practice for the promotion of a more flexible and supportive workforce (Salovey et al., 1999). Along with Daniel Goleman in the early 1990s there was a realisation about the usefulness of EI as a predictor of job performance. In 1998 Goleman wrote his best-selling book, *Working with Emotional Intelligence*. While teaching, Goleman realised the potential for EI drawing out characteristics that were over and above an often-used IQ label. He and colleagues often related how the students with the best grades were failing to hold down good jobs after graduation. His research, and that of his professor, confirmed that the so-called 'soft skills' of intelligent perception, anticipation, empathy and conflict resolution were more highly valued by employers. He quotes the senior company executive who was eminently well-qualified and worked long hours for the company but could not deal with the slightest confrontational issue with staff (Goleman, 1998, p40). One of the well-known facts among social work lecturers is that generally students who enter social work education with considerable experience are more able to make sense of this in relation to theory because they have concrete examples to which they can apply the theories they are learning. Knowing the intellectual constituents of the theory but having no examples to relate it to is of little use in interrogating the implications, potential responses, seating the interaction in the broader context of social constructionism or even in realising the empathy that might need to be applied to the situation.

Knowing Goleman's skill sets will enable you to recognise those you have and to develop those you don't.

Leading on from Howard Gardner's domains of the emotions, Goleman set about developing a more comprehensive list of competencies under two broad areas, those of personal

**Daniel Goleman's skill sets for EI**

| Personal Competence | Social Competence |
|---|---|
| Self-awareness – *emotional awareness, accurate self-assessment, self-confidence* | Social awareness – *empathy, service orientation, developing others, leveraging diversity, political awareness* |
| Self-regulation – *self control, trustworthiness, conscientiousness, adaptability, innovativeness* | Social skills – *influence, communication, leadership, change catalyst, conflict management, building bonds, collaboration and co-operation, team capabilities* |
| Self-motivation – *achievement drive, commitment, initiative, optimism* | |

competence and social competence. Within these areas he identified five domains, from which stemmed 25 sub themes and 93 competence descriptors.

To see Goleman's complete framework for EI in full, go to www.businessballs.com/emotional intelligencecompetencies.pdf

You may also like to 'meet' Daniel Goleman in an interview on YouTube at www.youtube.com/watch?v=NeJ3FFlyFye that was filmed on 13 March 2012.

Within the domain of personal competence and taking the theme of self-awareness and the first sub-theme in the competence descriptor of emotional awareness, let's look at some applications to social work.

Personal competence

Self-awareness

Emotional awareness

\* Know which emotions they are feeling and why

\* Realise the links between their feelings and what they think, do and say.

\* Recognise how their feelings affect their performance

\* Have a guiding awareness of their values and goals

---

*ACTIVITY* **5.2**

*Now re-read the case study of Mary on page 96. Apply the above competence descriptors to thinking about the work you are about to undertake with Mary and write your comments in your learning log.*

## Comment

Could you identify what you might feel and why? Were you angry at the conspiracy to deny Mary her children? Or were you apprehensive at the thought of opening up this complex case and unsure how you would manage it? How might these feelings cause you to promote or resist taking action?

Think about how you might broach the subject of Mary accessing her records and how you and other professionals could support her. How might you bring this issue to supervision with your practice educator? It is usually a good idea to have used this thinking to form some ideas, strategies and questions when you bring such complex cases to debate. Might it be useful to use the experience of your agency's staff group by presenting this case for debate?

---

**ACTIVITY 5.3**

*Secondly, let's take the second domain of social competence, and within that look at the theme of social awareness and the sub-theme of empathy. Again revisiting Mary's case, apply each of the competence descriptors and record your responses in your learning log.*

---

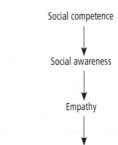

Social competence

↓

Social awareness

↓

Empathy

↓

\* Are attentive to emotional cues and listen well

\* Show sensitivity and understand others' perspectives

\* Help out based on understanding other people's needs and feelings

## Comment

What are some of the emotional cues you might expect to see from Mary? How would you portray good and non-judgemental listening skills? What do you think Mary's thoughts might be and how could you help her to understand the complexity of what you might reveal and to make decisions on what action she might want to take?

Remember that keeping these examples of reflective thinking in your learning log will be useful to you when completing your placement portfolio as they will enable you to practice thinking in these probing ways and prompt you to do the same while in placement.

These areas of EI are just a snapshot of the numerous descriptors and the remaining 86 are all equally relevant to social work practice. In understanding what these are and how you might respond to them you will be developing your abilities to use your multiple intelligences. As it has been shown by various research studies, the most successful employees use a synthesis of all these competences in the workplace, ensuring they are emotionally well adjusted, resilient, able to manage complexity, and to inspire and lead others by example.

Moving on to the third area in our triumvirate of intelligences, I want to introduce you to Appreciative Inquiry (AI) because this takes the personal, social and individual work you have now done into the workplace with a realisation of the strategies, skills and aptitudes that can be used to 'read' the nature and context therein. Not only that but AI can also be applied to work with service users to enable a focus on optimistic outcomes rather than problem-focused work.

# Appreciative Inquiry (AI)

AI is a strategic change method that was developed in the mid-1980s by David Cooperrider and Suresh Srivastva at Case Western University (2005). It is essentially a management initiative used in problem identification and solution that works with favourable critical judgement or opinion and in doing so searches for knowledge and information through questioning. It focuses on drawing out what is good about a situation and questions why this is so. While attempting to problem-solve there is a tendency to concentrate on what is wrong and see difficulties as to why it will be hard to fix. However, AI encourages a positive shift through using the **'5D approach'**: **Define** (the organisational change strategy); Discover (the best of what exists); **Dream** (what might be); **Design** (what should be); **Deliver/Destiny** (what will be). Here we see elements of future-basing – an organisational method of using time spacing to denote where we want to be in one week, three months or two years and which is often used with service users to envisage recovery/development. Also, there are links to Solution-focused Intervention – emphasising times of equilibrium and normality during times of crisis and uncertainty in a bid to recapture and return to the steady state.

Let's take each of the 5D domains and apply these to social work.

---

**ACTIVITY 5.4**

**The 5 Ds**

*You will remember Mary's case study earlier in this chapter. What you felt on reading her case file might initially be seen as a major problem in that it was a miscarriage of social justice to deny Mary her right to be a mother and her children their rights to be cared for by their birth mother.*

*Continued*

---

ACTIVITY 5.4 *Continued*

*Taking each of the five domains in turn (Define, Discover, Dream, Design/Destiny and Deliver), apply them to Mary's situation using the principles of AI. Try to write at least four responses to each using AI principles, for example:*

> *searching for knowledge and information through questioning while focusing on drawing out what is good about a situation and questioning why this is so.*

*Write your responses in your learning log for future reference.*

## Comment

Taking each of these domains I have suggested four questions that you might pose using the principles of AI.

## Define

1. What would be the organisational position and strategy for managing this process of discovery for Mary?

2. How might we cope with the emergent changes and the lack of clarity of outcome?

3. The process is suited to long-term change so I must appreciate my responsibility, once started, to support Mary through it as far as possible. I may need to carefully manage the transfer of the work to another service or worker if necessary.

4. How might we make use of systems both as a theory and as an interdisciplinary method?

## Discover

1. The best thing to discover is that Mary's children did not die at birth and it is likely that they could be traced through adoption services should Mary wish this to happen.

2. Her future may be very positive as she may have grandchildren and two families who may agree to become involved with her eventually.

3. I will need to discover how to work with Mary in order to give her insight about whether to access this information.

4. What might be the best way to sensitively address these issues with Mary, and what personnel and resources would I need to support the work?

This approach does not focus on the problems or wholly on negative risks, although these would be integral and need to be anticipated, but on what the solutions might be.

## Dream

1. What might Mary's view of her future be if she decides to access information about her children? She would need to consider the possibility that they may not wish to make contact with her.

2. How can I use the team/supervision/specialists to talk through the implications and question my own motives in the work?

3. How can I rationalise safe practice in not revealing knowledge of the information to Mary with the risky revelations in sharing information that may lead to joy or further heartache for her?

4. What new opportunities can I generate while acknowledging the risks to all involved?

You might decide not to take any action on the 'file'. If so, why have you made that decision and with what implications for Mary and her family? How might your unique situation affect your decision?

## Design/Destiny

1. What process would need to be developed in order to achieve the goal of Mary having knowledge of her family if she wishes?

2. What expertise could I draw on in the team to support this?

3. What systems of support could I draw around Mary to support her?

4. What theories would be appropriate to underpin the work?

If you decide to reveal to Mary the contents of her file you will move into the area of creating a social and procedural architecture required to realise the 'dreams'. This stage does not focus on the traditional approach of risk analysis, although these do need to be considered in all of the above questions and should underpin all the work done. However, they are carried through within the context of a positive driver rather than a negative blocker. Building systems of support, giving knowledge and information, minimises the effect of any inherent risks.

## Deliver

1. We may begin by establishing a life storybook approach to log Mary's wishes, feelings and desires. This should especially recognise when it will be important to pause.

2. I should look into whether Mary would benefit from having an independent advocate.

3. From a legal point of view Mary should be given information about her rights to access her case files and I need to check on the third party information to be removed prior to this.

4. A longer-term view may need me to access specialist information services, for example an adoption tracing agency.

The delivery phase gives opportunities to put into practice the visions and propositions of the dream and design stages. It is marked as a time of creative vision, continuous learning, adjustment and improvisation.

# What next?

Having reached the final stage, the whole process begins again with defining an issue – replicating the cyclical approach reminiscent of reflective practice. It is clear that risk, doubt, and problem identification are all involved in AI yet it is a way of opening up the mind to more critically evaluate new horizons using creativity and your unique 'self'. In the words of Watkins and Mohr, it is 'change at the speed of imagination' (Watkins and Mohr, 2001).

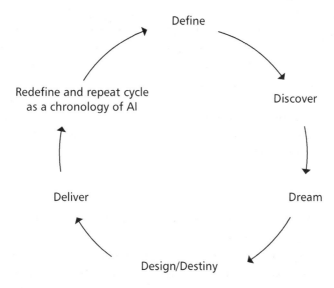

*Figure 5.1   The Appreciative Inquiry Cycle*

The authors of AI change management texts emphasise the journeying nature of their work, such that the work is never set in stone but fluid and open to individual interpretation, flexibility and evolution. Similarly, EI stresses the collaborative nature of social and emotional learning and the presence of resonant approaches – being on the same wavelength – in touch with others' feelings, ideas, emotions and showing empathy, self-awareness and self-regulation through being motivated to use one's own talents towards negotiation and persuasion within social networks. Underpinning these two approaches and their plethora of attributes, Howard Gardner offers us a new look at what constitutes our intellectual abilities – namely, that IQ is but a small measurable part of the abilities we possess.

---

**CHAPTER SUMMARY**

The complexity of, say, the spatial and musical intelligences of Gardner, the application of self-awareness and social skills from Goleman with the 5D approach of Cooperrider and Whitney lead the consummate social work practitioner into a process of artistic creativity worthy of any highly praised theatrical production. Yet the stage direction is often not within their gift but it remains the province of the agency within which they work or in the thoughts and actions of the service users they are working with. As such,

*Continued*

---

**CHAPTER SUMMARY** *Continued*

then, this highly complex process, called social work, is impossible to define simply as it is through the interplay between a myriad of human emotions, theories, systems, politics and social change mechanisms that, as individual practitioners, we negotiate our roles. The ability to question and articulate our responses to such social themes enables us to establish our professional integrity and to bear the emotional content of the work. It is with this intellectual aura that we move into Chapter 6 to examine the development of the critical practitioner. As a beginning practitioner you will decide where you are up to in your development and be comfortable in what you know you can do. That does not mean you should become complacent or that your working practices lead to stagnation. Instead, you will be testing out new areas of knowledge in practice, developing new intelligences and applying your skills to the agency appreciatively as potential mentors, practice educators or leaders. If you would like to read more about the psychology of the emotions, then David Howe's book would be useful to you, particularly Chapter 10, 'The Practitioner Relationship and Emotional Intelligence'.

**FURTHER READING**

**Goleman, D** (1998) *Working with emotional intelligence.* London: Bloomsbury.

The text is a sequel to Goleman's 1996 text on Emotional Intelligence and it drives his ideas on EI into newly emerging workforce situations. His lively and amusing examples add to the accessible nature of the book and lead us to focus on how we manage ourselves and others through emotions rather than by waving certificates and intelligence quotients. His numerous skill categories and attribute lists are clear and highly applicable to social work practice and life in general.

**Howe, D (2008)** *The emotionally intelligent social worker.* Basingstoke: Palgrave Macmillan.

A comprehensive text that extensively documents the emotional elements that complement knowledge, skills, experience, values and beliefs within social work practice. The book gives a good grounding into EI for social work and also fuses this with explanations of how it can be an important consideration in a variety of medical, psychosocial and neuro-pathological conditions.

**USEFUL WEBSITES**

**www.eiconsortium.org/reports/what_is_emotional_intelligence.html**

The site contains a useful article by Cary Cherniss entitled 'Emotional Intelligence: What is it and why it matters'. You can also find guidelines for best practice in EI, and the EI competence framework on **www.eiconsortium.org** on the black header, just click on 'reports'.

**http://howardgardner01.files.wordpress.com/2012/06/intro-frames-10-23-10.pdf**

This site gives you access to Howard Gardner's thoughts on 'Multiple Intelligences – The first thirty years' in which he details how the concept has influenced human potential, and will continue to impact on professional life within the new world order.

**www.iisd.org/ai/**

This website of the International Institute for Sustainable Development offers useful insight into how AI can be used for community development. The principles and application of AI in this example are suitable for smaller scale group and community work development within the social work field.

# Chapter 6
## Developing as a critical practitioner

A C H I E V I N G   A   S O C I A L   W O R K   D E G R E E

This chapter will help you to develop the following capabilities, to the appropriate level, from the **Professional Capabilities Framework**:

- **Professionalism**
Describe the importance of emotional resilience in social work.

- **Values and ethics**
Understand the profession's ethical principles and their relevance to practice.

- **Critical reflection and analysis**
Recognise and describe why evidence in important in social work practice.

- **Intervention and skills**
Demonstrate core communication skills and capacity to develop them. Demonstrate the ability to engage with people in order to build compassionate and effective relationships.

It will also introduce you to the following standards as set out in the 2008 social work subject benchmark statement:

4.2    Social work involves the critical application of research knowledge to inform understanding and to underpin action, reflection and evaluation.

5.1.1 Social work services, service users and carers.

5.1.2 The service delivery context.

5.1.4 Social work theory.

5.2    Subject specific skills and other skills.

5.5.1 Managing problem-solving activities.

5.5.3 Analyse and synthesise knowledge gathered for problem-solving.

5.8    Challenge unacceptable practices in a responsible manner.

6.2    Practice skills and experience.

7.3    Knowledge and understanding.

7.4    Subject-specific and other skills.

## Introduction

In Chapter 4 I made reference to the fact that doing social work entails much more than doing a job. I spoke of *human flourishing* and *transformational learning*. These are attributes that indicate to us that while in training, pursuing an education and in practice, social work students can expect to be changed. I mentioned the idea that an understanding of virtue ethics should lead you to a fundamental and central belief that you should practise with the best possible intentions as to do otherwise would make you dissatisfied and uncomfortable. This means using intelligence and legitimate authority; taking responsibility and being accountable; using an up-to-date knowledge base while integrating values and beliefs commensurate with the social work codes of practice and beyond. In this chapter I am going to take these ideas further in relating the human dilemma of morality and virtue between the personal and the professional life, the application of emotional intelligence and appreciative inquiry, and set these ideas within the cultural context of social work today.

In offering you some examples, activities and comments, I hope the highly complex integration of these ideas and practices will enable you to begin to see the nature of social work as a shifting and contested practice, and consequently to begin to develop your fitness to practise within it.

By the end of this chapter you will be able to:

- apply the language of critical practice;
- apply the constituents of emotional intelligence to your practice;
- be able to identify your personal attributes that are valuable to social work;
- appreciate the nature of challenge, courage and self-control in social work;
- be able to use skills of collaboration, political awareness and influence in your agency practice.

# What's in a name – the language of critical practice?

Various writers have recently given us terms with which to develop our thinking about critical practice. Fook and Askeland (2007) differentiate between reflective practice and critical reflection on practice. They claim that the latter is somehow both broader and deeper than the former, incorporating emancipatory, political and social justice ideas. However, Thompson and Thompson (2008) make a claim for reflective practice that inherently must contain a critical perspective as not to do so could lead to dangerous practice:

> *for example, by unwittingly reinforcing patterns of discrimination.*

> (Thompson and Thompson, 2008, p27)

Dalrymple and Burke (1995) situate the process of change within assessment as being something that affects both practitioners and service users, saying:

> *we can be in the positions of Participant and Observer which has been described as reflexivity.*

> (in Jones et al., 2007, p112)

Reflexive practice, then, is said to be different from reflective practice in that it causes us to evaluate our position within our practice from a personal involvement perspective and recognises that practitioners are subject to change and continuity through the impact of the interchange. Alternatively, Schön (1986) refers to this as 'reflection-in-action' while retrospective 'reflection-on-action' comes after the event.

A more radical definition of reflexivity is proposed by Webb (2006) as:

> *Reflexivity means a confrontation with self-identity. In social work terms if a reflective practitioner is one who thinks carefully and critically about her or his own practice, a reflexive practitioner is engaged in radical confrontation with the very ethical basis and legitimation of practice and self-involvement. In other words, as we shall see, reflexive practice introduces an important moral dimension into social work that is lacking in the reflective practitioner literature.*

(Webb, 2006, p36)

# Critical practitioners in the making

This is confusing, isn't it? The ideas appear to be difficult enough without contesting definitions about what they actually mean. Yet this is the theatre of professional life – the shifting and contested nature of practice, and as we see, that also applies to theory in practice too. Try to come to an understanding of what critical reflection means to you as a practitioner and then use that definition. I feel the definition by Webb (2006) is quite radical and wonder whether it is practical to use this all the time. We might say that reflective, reflexive and critical practice are a triumvirate of domains that we would need to embrace in developing as a critical practitioner. However, not all need to be in play all of the time and they may have different functions and be for different audiences. Figure 6.1 might help you to see where each of these terms fits, but it is just my idea and not written in stone.

Although I have separated these terms for clarity of definition, they are not so easily divided in practice. For example, you could say that in reflecting you also critique the morality of removing a person's freedom because they display different behaviours. What would make this more reflexive is where you also consider the implications of not doing so – vulnerability of service users, wrath of the press and relatives if you do not take action or fear for your own job if you did take action. You might also stress that you would need to consider your

| Type of practice | Function | Example |
|---|---|---|
| Reflective | Use after or during the event to analyse professional activity. | In supervision. During a practice session In discussion with colleagues. As part of a portfolio narrative of your practice. |
| Reflexive | Use before, during and/or after the event to critique the morality and virtue ethics of the event. | Respond to service users. Challenge self and others about the reasons and outcomes for/of the event. |
| Critical | Use before, during and after the event to critique personal and professional histories, practice and the social construction of problems. | Digest the discourse of the personal and the private, the creation of 'others' and the binaries of power that exist to discriminate and oppress. Disseminate your thinking through presentations, conference papers and/or publications. |

*Figure 6.1 Integrating levels of critical practice*

own feelings of altruism in making a defensible assessment and judgement. Critically, you could draw on the history of incarceration as at times for punishment or protection, socially constructed as dangerous or vulnerable and subject to mass hysteria (mentally ill man murders mother and child) or reproach (elderly mentally ill grandmother dies alone).

Interacting with service users, you would be monitoring and evaluating your responses; with your supervisor/mentor you might, in addition to justifying your actions, be posing questions that the interaction raises for you and your agency. At the same time you could be making connections between the theory of social constructionism and discourse analysis in an attempt to push your learning to deeper levels ready for preparing a conference paper or journal article. These activities may be triggered by one interaction in practice or by something you read or observe, overhear, or a debate you take part in whether in the professional forum or while standing at the photocopier or having a lunch break.

You might be able to make some comparisons here with your practice as 'professional artistry' that I mentioned in Chapter 4. You are not simply carrying out tick lists, or applying the minimum effort and analysis to your work, but always seeing that there is additional learning and understanding to be gained by 'going the extra mile'.

---

ACTIVITY **6.1**

*Suppose you are working in a mental health setting and one of your service users needs hospital treatment but is prepared to go only as a voluntary inpatient. There are only emergency compulsory beds available and so she will have to wait a week. Her neighbour is constantly telephoning you to complain about your service user's behaviour as it is keeping her awake all night and she is afraid of her violent outbursts that are increasingly being visited upon her. The complaining neighbour is threatening to go to the police and press if something isn't done urgently. What do you do?*

*Write down what action you might take and why, followed by the consequences for all stakeholders.*

---

## Comment

You might empathise with the neighbour, saying that you are doing all you can and as soon as possible your service user will receive treatment. Or you might think, what are the implications of this situation for the service user's neighbour? How might I alleviate the tension that is building up without further exacerbating things for the service user? A Masters student I was supervising once had this dilemma. She resolved it by presenting her care manager with a plan to offer the neighbour a weekend holiday in Blackpool. She presented her evidence – that the service user was in danger of being involved in confrontation that may have serious consequences, that the neighbour was contemplating calling in the police and press because social services were 'rubbish', and that there was a potential to do good in changing attitudes about 'the welfare' in the community. She also considered that the service user would be likely to suffer detriment as police involvement could promote a compulsory admission. She won her case, the neighbour enjoyed a short holiday and her service user was admitted to a voluntary bed within seven days where she received appropriate treatment.

The student demonstrated that she was a critical practitioner by imagining an unusual solution, marshalling her evidence and presenting a coherent and convincing case to her care manager.

It is this ability to **define, discover and dream** that was discussed in Chapter 5 using Appreciative Inquiry (AI). In an uncertain situation the student used her Emotional Intelligence (EI) skills to challenge the system by being able to envisage the potential consequences to all stakeholders; the neighbour, service user, social work agency and herself as the social worker. Using AI, she **designed** response showing what the **destiny** was to be in this situation, albeit an unusual one, that was outside the normal static thinking of the system but presented her case evidence convincingly using her EI skills. Finally, using AI, the outcome or delivery of the engagement was achieved by her activating the organisational systems to achieve the plan. Central to her plan was her ability to present a 'provocative proposition' through the 'conversational process'. These are two elements that Lewis et al. (2008) propose as central to AI and the process of using the World Café as an organisational change process.

Now you can use your critical practitioner skills to work on this case example.

---

### ACTIVITY 6.2

*Read the following case study and, using critical thinking skills, write down how you might handle this situation.*

*Next draw out the proposals you think you can create a good case for and list the most convincing points. If you really want to develop your critical thinking you might take this a step further by imagining what reaction you might receive from your colleagues and care manager. Don't forget to put all the material you generate into your critical learning log.*

---

### CASE STUDY

*My placement involved me in working with service users with learning disabilities with psychosocial needs that required intensive behavioural management. Perhaps because of the case of dealing with clients with challenging behaviour, my team consisted mainly of male staff.*

*I found working in a male-dominated team trying at times. I grew tired of some of the comments and sexist assumptions that were commonly made. On many occasions I witnessed an oppressive use of language about women, for example 'boys will be boys, but one day all girls will be women'; 'why do women have small feet? – so they can get closer to the sink!' All used in an assuming joking way.*

*Continued*

---

**CASE STUDY** *Continued*

*Dilemmas*

*I found it difficult to challenge these sexist comments, and quickly realised that it was difficult to do this without making myself a target for ridicule. I chose to keep silent in many instances ... when I tried to challenge it, I was attacked for being oversensitive, uptight or 'feminazi'. I tried to take my concerns to my practice teacher, who said that all men just 'like to have a laugh'. The notion of femininity and masculinity of the organisation where I was placed were just assumptions about the nature of men and women. The assumptions that were drawn upon excluded or undervalued the work of women. Many of my colleagues and their ideas of womanhood were related to family or domestic life, and of men to public life. As an example I was expected to do most of the cooking and cleaning, and was responsible for overall management of the house. This has consequences for the development of gendered, organisational culture. I identified several conflicting situations. For example, the service users (who were male) responded to females in the organisation in terms of expectations associated with sex and roles, and taking normality for granted, reinforcing stereotypical expectations of women as 'natural' carers. The link between the male stereotype and the values that dominated the nature of the organisation were evident – for example, the notion that to deal with challenging behaviour you need to be rational, analytic, strategic, decision-oriented, tough and aggressive just as men are. Women were seen as everything best suited to the traditional female roles assuming inferiority. When they (myself included) broke out of these roles we were accused of being 'overly assertive' and trying to 'play a male role'.*

---

## Comment

You might like to create a framework to follow. For example, you could begin by writing down all the implications you think the situation might have for the service users, the student, colleagues and the agency. Then, stemming from each of these postulate (think about and propose) some possible solutions. Don't worry if they seem a little wacky – a weekend in Blackpool was not what was normally envisaged by the student's care manager!

Finally, draw out the proposals you think you can create a good case for and list the most convincing points. If you really want to develop your critical thinking you might take this a step further by imagining what reaction you might receive from your colleagues and care manager.

This piece of critical practice stemmed from a female student who was working in an all-male agency with all-male service users. She was subject to sexist jokes and language, and it was made clear to her that she should make tea and wash up. She felt very uncomfortable every day she went to work and began to dread each day. She struggled with whether she should withdraw from her placement but also felt that it was against her principles to 'give in'. She clearly used the language of being in a fight with her agency colleagues and the service users.

In a moment of feeling angry with herself for feeling so powerless, she began to relate back to a lecture on feminist theory at the university. She was able to relate the idea of the social construction of women as nurturers, and as passive, gentle and submissive beings subject to irrationality (probably due to biological differences); whereas male attributes seemed to be related to dominance, order, thrusting control, authority and rationality. She began to see that men were not to be blamed for this (she had been using a lot of energy on this) because they were as much victims of the social construction of gender as were women.

She wrote down her thoughts in a learning narrative and began to use this to construct a case that she would use in supervision with the agency service manager. She used theoretical references, journal articles and practice summaries to support her arguments for how she was feeling. At the end of supervision she offered to meet with the staff group to do a presentation and this was agreed. She also related this to the National Occupational Standards so that she could use it as evidence of her competence.

The all-male staff group were impressed with her presentation and some felt upset because they hadn't realised what effect they had on her. Some said they had just been joking and she had taken things too seriously, taking a 'blame the victim' stance.

She reiterated the legitimacy of her feelings and an agreement was made to cease their behaviour. Of course she could not prevent them thinking sexist thoughts but she could monitor their behaviour while in the workplace. Some of the staff offered to help her in facilitating the group.

In her critical reflection the student castigated herself for allowing the situation to continue to such an extent that it almost caused her to give up a good placement. She now realised the power of using theory in practice and of dealing with unpleasant situations quickly without allowing them to fester. She was also able to see that she had much to contribute to experienced practitioners and began to gain confidence in her own abilities to change the status quo.

Here is how she represented her growth.

---

**CASE STUDY**

*Reflection and growth in practice*

*I became aware of the disadvantaged position of women with mental ill health, and the effect for some of not being a fit enough mother to care for their children. In a society where parenting is seen primarily as mothering, poor parenting, neglect or abuse are therefore constructed mainly as a failure on the part of women. I can now see that concepts of 'normality' are gendered. I am aware that social work can been seen to reinforce sexism if a critical approach is not adopted, and sexism can also be seen to be a major factor underpinning many of the problems social workers are asked to tackle.*

*Continued*

*Sexism is closely linked to the concept of patriarchy and Weber (1998) used this concept to refer to the dominance of men within the family. Its use has been extended to refer to the dominance of men in general, as reflected in the distribution of power in society. Sexism is a set of beliefs, practices and institutional structures that reinforces and is reinforced by patriarchy. I also asked my tutor for some references about feminist practice and now use these to support my arguments for men to change their practice.*

*One particular day I expressed my anger. Some men in the team became very defensive but to my surprise and relief two of my male colleagues were very supportive and made strenuous attempts to rid the team of its sexist tendencies. I now feel well equipped for my practice as a social worker having experienced sexism and having the knowledge to know how to challenge dominant discriminatory attitudes, values, practices and structures.*

# Emancipatory and transformative potential

In the above example the student began to see herself as confident and capable of influencing the views of powerful others. She learned that from a position of disempowerment and victimisation she was able to create an agenda that was within her control rather than that of her oppressors. Further, she realised that perhaps in order to move through learning barriers she needed to experience adversity and from that emerged feelings of affirmation and capability. She had been able to take on what Mezirow terms a 'perspective transformation' (1991). She had effectively used a narrative therapy to construct new meanings out of her situation and in the process not only empowered herself but also the men on bail who had assaulted women. This type of critical reflection is called 'emancipatory' because it 'transforms' the victim out of their given role and frees them up to new 'agency'. Using the role of 'actors' on the stage of work, private life, leisure and education, individuals are able to strengthen their social capital by using critically reflective practice in this manner.

# Revisiting Emotional Intelligence (EI)

In Chapter 5 the notion of EI would have opened up for you ideas about the usefulness of the 'softer' emotional skills integral to your work. These were complementary to knowledge, values, beliefs and increasingly seen as central to social work practice. Not only that, but the application of EI domains is equally important within our personal lives and across a plethora of trades, professions and social encounters. In other words, EI is axiomatic in the journey towards becoming a virtuous practitioner, colleague and friend.

In an article about developing EI in the workplace, Nicholas Clarke undertook research in UK hospices and analysed data taken from healthcare professionals (Clarke, 2006). He deduced that the development of EI through dialogue and reflection with colleagues, for example through a journal club, was due to the search for a professional identity. Indeed, the very diverse nature of what constitutes social work does lead us to tremble when asked *So what is social work?* The skills set and values of social work lend themselves to the development of EI and, when coupled with the knowledge base and HCPC Professional Capabilities Framework, should give social work a distinct place with which to define itself as a profession. It is in the application of a series of 'lenses' through which to view social work that we now apply EI to Critical Learning and your development as a critical practitioner.

---

**ACTIVITY 6.3**

*Now I want you to respond to this critical incident log report by writing down how you think an uncritical student might have reacted. This means you will be thinking through what constitutes poor practice in order to recognise it in yourself and others. Having recognised such practice you will be more able to deal with it and to see it as identifying areas for improvement through self-critique rather than ignoring something that you see as personal criticism.*

*Keep your responses in your log.*

---

**CASE STUDY**

### Critical event

*I was assisting the volunteer co-ordinator to interview a 56-year-old white woman, who has difficulty walking and has to take strong medication to control diabetes and other conditions. She wanted to come on the ten-week in-house training course. She had worked in welfare rights for years but was involved in a very bad car accident two years previously. She was also a carer for her mother.*

*I felt she was lacking in people skills and would be difficult to work with in a team. She said that if she had to work in a miserable team she would leave the interview. She said that people who had degrees were 'often thick' and I felt resentful about her comment because I have worked so hard on mine. Her attitude was one of indifference. I had to question her more than other candidates. Some of her documentation had different forenames. She appeared to me to be taking over the interview.*

### Dilemmas

*The co-ordinator said I had acted in a discriminatory way, completely taken over the interview and excluded her input. I was shocked by this. She asked why the candidate's comments had affected me so much. I realised that I was feeling raw because I had a lot going on in my personal life and I still had to study and be on placement. I felt she was being unfair and had to refrain from getting angry. She suggested I had overreacted and I became adamant that I had not. She explained that during the interview my manner and body language was so different from the way I normally communicate with people that she noticed it and wondered what was wrong. I challenged the co-ordinator and said that the woman would not fit in with a healthy team. She said that was true but the training would have helped her. I felt this was too 'soft' and relations between us became strained.*

## Comment

An uncritical practitioner would have retained the anger caused by the initial practice teacher's comments. Maybe she would have stuck to her decision that the volunteer was not a fit person to work in the agency. She would have failed to appreciate that the experience of the practice teacher was being given freely in an attempt to guide her learning. She would have been closed to alternative thinking and the views of anyone but her own. She would have mistakenly thought that being dogmatic having once made her decision was a sign of strength. She would not have understood the art of compromise, lateral thinking or used her emotional intelligence.

So what do you think she actually did? Here is her account.

---

**CASE STUDY**

*Reflection, growth in practice*

*I began to reflect on the interview and the part I had played in that. I thought about my own life and everything that had been going on in it and I suddenly realised that I had made no allowances for the interviewee's social circumstances, which had been obviously difficult for her. Further I had failed to see that she was vulnerable and defensive rather than offensive and possibly was responding to my own behaviour. With hindsight I could see that she had a lot of skills to offer. I needed to reflect on the fact that whether I like or dislike someone can really affect my judgement in working with people and this means that I am not delivering an equal service. I potentially excluded this woman from making progress when she had been so ill. When the realisation of these facts hit me, I felt horrible and could not believe my thinking had been so judgemental and closed. Here was a mindset that needed to be changed for future good practice. I recognised that the personal and professional cross and merge with each other and become the same. I decided to take action and be honest about the experience. I explained all this to the co-ordinator and asked if she would help me to develop some strategies for dealing with situations such as those and identified it as a significant learning need. The fact that I was challenged by the worker was paramount to my own professional development and I now realise how necessary and valuable it is to have good supervision.*

---

The student was shocked by the comments from her practice teacher and this provided a catalyst for change. She reflected on the experience and accepted that her behaviour had indeed been discriminatory. The volunteer candidate was herself a victim of attitudes to do with illness and health, gender and class. What did the student do that demonstrated her abilities as a 'critical practitioner'?

- She opened up her practice to scrutiny.

- She recognised what she thought was good practice and justified this on the grounds that she was validating someone who would work with vulnerable service users.

- She was prepared to question this practice in light of adverse comments from her practice teacher.

- She reframed the experience as one she could learn from, so taking the anger and embarrassment out of it.

- She realised that events happening in her personal life had largely impacted on the situation.

- She revisited her value base and her beliefs about the power she possessed as a (student) social worker.

- She made suggestions about how she could further develop her practice.

- She took this learning into her practice for the future in that she would learn how to balance the rights of both service users and volunteers within the agency's policy of promoting service user involvement.

We could excavate each of these traits separately by their constituent parts. Goleman helps us with this. He adds further attributes and behaviours that he sees as the essence of EI. Here are some of his and some of mine that I have put into the following categories.

| | |
|---|---|
| To do with character | Initiative, adaptability, self-awareness, persuasiveness, self-confidence, drive optimism, sensitivity, inspiration. |
| To do with values | Trustworthiness, self-control, integrity, conscientiousness, political awareness. |
| To do with beliefs | Commitment, cultivating alliances, insight for change, nurture, co-operation, honesty. |
| To do with a skill set | Empathy, innovation, developing others, anticipating, using influence, listening, conflict management, resolution-focused, collaboration, creating synergy to achieve goals through team work, being able to read others. |

Can you see how we began with the language of critical practice, moved on to the levels and courage of risk and control, affirmation and confidence, and now the character, beliefs, values and skill sets? Critical practice is all of these things, but is it all of them all of the time? Alternatively, does a 'critical mass' occur when a few coalesce into a synthesis of practice?

# Critical mass

Critical mass is what Goleman refers to when he discusses the idea that top professional performers possess attributes and behaviours across all the above domains and in the coming together of these display an emotional intelligence that excels. So we can say that in order to develop as a critical practitioner you must demonstrate that you have a good grasp of most of the above values, beliefs and skills, and in addition that you have taken on board, as did our volunteer-assessing student, that you need to address changes in your very character. When these changes come together they cause a shift in your essence, the very essential nature of who you are as a professional person. Not only that, but these newly acquired attributes change who you are as a private person too. Some students have mentioned this coming together of several attributes as *like a penny dropping, a light went on*, everything became clear. They had a problem and were searching for the solution but were unable to fill the gap, join up the wiring or plug into the right socket. Suddenly their internal wiring became connected and they were able to see the way to act to bring about a solution. Sometimes they were more able to deal with not being able to see the solution but only to identify more difficulties, like the fog clearing on a sea journey only to reveal rocks in the ship's path. The crucial element is how they needed to think about their situation in order for change to occur. Just like biological theories of synergy and change, the whole has become more than its constituent parts, rather like average individual singers who together in a choir can achieve the most amazing success.

---

### ACTIVITY 6.4

*Look at the following examples of critical practitioner development.*

1. *The student who felt embarrassed and uncomfortable until she challenged the homophobic jokes of her classmates.*
2. *The worker who explained to his own child why the terms 'spastic' and 'gay' that seemed to be sexy in adolescent parlance had actually come from oppressing people in those categories.*
3. *The mental health day-centre organiser who invited local residents and service users to a discussion held in her own home when local opposition to enlargement of the centre threatened to stop the project.*

*Taking each of these examples in turn, match the attributes from the character, values, beliefs and skills sets with the three examples above.*

---

## Comment

You will have to put yourself in the position of the 'actor' in each case and imagine the thinking processes that each might have used. You might choose to represent these as a framework for each example, as follows.

|  | Character | Values | Beliefs | Skill |
|---|---|---|---|---|
| Example 1 | self-awareness | integrity | insight | empathy |
|  | sensitivity | political | honesty | developing others |
|  | initiative | awareness |  |  |

What you are doing is to anticipate in each situation how you might develop this critical mass by anticipating the unseen thinking behind these actions. This student was self-aware in that she felt the physical impact of discriminatory remarks. She was sensitive to her own feelings and knew she had to do something to change this. Sometimes we need to put ourselves in difficult situations because we just know that we cannot rest until we have made some effort to change the status quo – however small. We feel more content when we have done this and our sense of integrity is congruent with the honesty of our feelings. Issues can be termed contentious or not by the differing and shifting discourses that infuse them. For example, we know that gender determinism is now a contested subject and to use gay people as the butt of jokes is unacceptable. It was not always so and within quite recent memory there was a strong lobby to create separate communities for gay men who had Aids. In this case the student was aware of the political discourse and it was seated in her value base. In challenging her classmates she was sharing her insight about their behaviour and expressing how she honestly felt. The way in which we challenge can either alienate or illuminate others and by using emotional intelligence she would have claimed the feelings as her own but demonstrated how the others might come to view their own remarks. She was in that way developing more political awareness, sensitivity and empathy in others. This is a really good activity for you to continue with, as it will help you to put Goleman's attributes and behaviours into practice. When you have completed the framework for each example, try writing a reflective explanation as I have done here. Put all this in your reflective log. You should feel that these activities make you think deeply, but why do you need to do that?

## The how and the why

What we have done so far is to think about how you might develop yourself as a critical practitioner. Generally, when we ask ourselves questions in order to improve our professional functioning it is about how we might do so. A critical practitioner will also be thinking why are those questions the right or wrong ones to ask, why do I think that is the correct course of action and why do I agree or have concerns about what others are doing/saying? Why might that action be contentious and why do I think in certain ways about people, even when I have no prior knowledge of them? Why does the way I was socialised cause me to think in certain ways about things and why do I find it difficult to accept criticism and challenge?

Initially, you might recognise that you really have no knowledge why and are happy to go with so-called 'gut feelings' and 'biological hunches' – the elation of meeting a loved one or stomach churning of meeting a troublesome friend. These instinctive feelings don't go away, even for the commensurate critical professional, but you will become more objective about how you interpret them through using your critical skills. Howe (2008) rather rejects the notion of instinct as being without thought yet these feelings play a large part in influencing how we think and act.

## Knowing and using your inner resources

Developing an ability to understand why you react and think as you do is part of a recognition of your own inner resources. As an inexperienced lecturer in HE, I was always nervous around one particular experienced colleague. I would try to befriend the person, to engage in conversation and to placate their cursory and often rude responses to my efforts. I was discussing my annoyance at my feelings and behaviour with another colleague and asked if they could suggest any strategies to help. Their suggestion was to ask me what I would like to do. I said that I felt I had made these overtures because it was important to me that I was accepted into the staff group but I was losing patience in extending the hand of friendship. I would really like just to ignore this colleague whenever possible. My critical friend said that the staff group already accepted me. That comment immediately gave me the confidence I had been lacking and I was able to have a conversation with myself where I celebrated the person I was rather than the person I was trying to be. Trying to second-guess how I needed to change had shattered my congruence and I was trying to be something I was not. Furthermore, I began to be able to use evidence to challenge assumptions that were being made about me. Critical thinking can lead us to open up self-doubt and this is a good thing because it leads us to really examine why we think and act as we do. However, personal evaluations that lead to affirmation are essential to our professional growth. Just like a child who is praised for small advances, we gain confidence and the ability to take risks if we know that our peers value us. Similarly, when taking an adversarial stance with colleagues we need to be aware of our effect upon them and focus on the potential for development rather than conflict.

---

### ACTIVITY 6.5

*Think about one attribute that you have which is valuable to you as a social worker. Sometimes it is good to ask a critical friend this question, as we don't always realise the positive things about ourselves as others see us.*

*Now think about an area of difficulty you have. This could be in accepting criticism or that you lack confidence in some situations. How can you deal with this using your positive attribute and therefore change a weakness into strength?*

---

### Comment

You might revisit the student narrative in Chapter 4, Activity 4.3, to remind you of the ways she dealt with criticism from her practice teacher.

# Challenge, courage and putting one's head above the parapet

In a student's critical reflections on his practice he mentioned a revelational moment when he had attended a meeting with his care manager who was also his supervisor. For months he had supervision with this man as his practice educator and their relationship was amicable yet rather mundane. He didn't feel particularly challenged in supervision and felt that if he kept his head down he would pass the placement. The student's practice educator was chairing the meeting. The subject was highly contentious and there were lots of opposition, conflicting information and confrontational behaviour. It would have been easy for the practice educator to take a soft option but instead he managed individuals, listened and responded to anxieties and differing points of view, focused on solutions rather than problems, compromised where appropriate and presented evidence to refute spurious claims. In effect, his emotional intelligence was fully engaged not only in the meeting but it was obvious that he had prepared well, understood the implications of the decisions to be made and was able to reach a plan of action where each participant felt their input was reflected. This observation profoundly affected the student and he vowed that this was a role model he wanted to follow. He felt imbued with admiration and confidence in his practice educator and decided to ask if he could role-play some situations that he felt he was lacking in during their next supervision session. As adults we often learn best by watching someone in action rather than reading about the theory of how it should be done. You might like to use this technique with your practice teacher or lecturer.

Recent practice gives a good example of how courage is involved in our everyday lives as social workers. A local news report (*Oldham Advertiser,* 11 September 2008) headlined *Mystery man now has real name and family* (Ottewell and Marsden) told the story of an older man who had been in residential care for eight years after being found in a 'dazed state' in the town centre. He was unable to give his consent for an appeal for informa-tion about his identity and the Council were unable to take the matter further until the law changed in October 2007. The legal department of the local council were then able to construct a defence should a case be brought under the Human Rights Act, although they still did not have the right to make decisions on his behalf. They decided to take a risk and contacted the local newspaper and a television programme. The man's son – who had pre-viously been told by the police that his father was dead – saw the programme.

What part do you think the social worker played in this? The fiscal imperative to discover relatives could be to recoup funding, to allocate responsibility and to ensure someone would meet funeral costs. The human imperative to belong to a family, to be reunited after past difficulties and to meet again a father who you thought was dead would be strongly motivational for a social worker. In addition, the two, father and son, are now working together daily to try to piece together a life through lost memories. However, the result could have been worse: recriminations, guilt, revenge and abuse might have resulted. So in instigating a chain of actions the social worker would have had to realise the potential consequences for a man who was unable to give his consent. The nature of this would impact upon the older man, his found family, the agency, the police (who previously declared him dead) and herself as his social worker. Do you think it might have been easier for the worker to continue with things as they were? Using courage to chal-lenge decisions, or the lack of them, is one of the value-based qualities that social workers possess. It is this attention to the human elements of bureaucratic organisations that gives social work a particular place within professional practice and which allows us a special position to argue the case for social work as a profession. It is also the area in which social workers need absolute support from their managers if they are to have the strength to stand and make decisions involving risk.

# Self-control and not doing one's duty

There is nothing more stimulating than taking a risky stance, promoting action from it and achieving a good outcome. One might say the social worker in the above case could have congratulated herself on a successful outcome. However, life is not straightforward, but messy and at the mercy of human subjects. Suppose there were powerful arguments for not proceeding to a public appeal. The worker could easily have felt ignored, that her professional status was not recognised and that her practice would have to be attuned and scaled down for future interventions. She may have felt that she was failing in her duty to reunite this man with his family. How might she have had to control her responses to being denied the power to act as she thought fit? She could have provided the 'mystery man' with opportunities to access his past by other means. One solution would be to focus on the values of 'belonging', having 'community presence', knowing who you are and who you were and how these might be provided by other means. In this way the worker is seeing the denial as an opportunity for further, lateral, thinking, rather than as a personal invalidation of her practice. Valuing people through reminiscence therapy, weekend placements into families and 'adopt a grandparent' initiatives would all be creative ways of providing belonging and community presence. This is providing there is recognition of the risk that remembering past lives can bring.

Goleman (1998) defines self-control as being able to keep disruptive emotions and impulses in check through managing feelings, staying focused and thinking clearly while under pressure (p82). He includes self-control as part of a suite of competencies of self-mastery. Trustworthiness, conscientiousness, adaptability and innovation complete the suite.

Here is a case example from a student on placement from where examples from the self-mastery suite can be drawn.

---

**ACTIVITY 6.6**

*In a substance-misuse residential setting and during a group therapy session one member of the group states that her partner, who is currently looking after the couple's children, regularly hits them because they are very naughty. In the same evening the resident receives an anonymous phone call to say that her house is on fire. Due to the probability of relapse behaviours, residents are not allowed to leave the setting during their course of treatment.*

1. *Imagine you are the group social worker and write down all your immediate thoughts on the issue.*
2. *Next write down what might be the implications of these events and thoughts for you as a social worker.*
3. *Devise a plan of action to incorporate as many of the emotional intelligence competencies as you can. As you write, put a small sign to indicate which of the intelligences you are evidencing.*
4. *Finally, anticipate potential implications and timescale that each element of your plan will have on the service user.*

---

## Comment

I will illustrate just one element here but I expect you will have written many more.

An initial thought could be that the service user will be very shocked by the anonymous phone call and unable to concentrate on dealing with the disclosure about her partner hitting the children. This might be left until she is more able to focus [sensitivity, nurture].

A major implication would be that she would be concerned for the safety of the children and her partner and would need reassurance either way [empathy, anticipating, ability to read others].

The initial plan would be to verify the authenticity of the phone call. You might do this by assisting her in making a phone call to a neighbour or friend and asking for the facts. You could contact the fire brigade or police to verify that this event had taken place and whether there was anyone injured [initiative, self-control, co-operation, resolution-focused].

The implications for the service user would be that she would be supported in ascertaining the facts, have information upon which to base future action and be in an environment where she would receive support from the social worker and other colleagues [initiative, integrity, conscientiousness, trustworthiness, honesty, resolution-focused, developing others].

This piece of work would be achievable within a short space of time, perhaps one hour, to focus on the next, and vital, part to ascertain the extent to which the children were subject to physical punishment.

# Resisting pressure

The critical practitioner is able to hold on to pressing issues, in this case potential physical abuse of children, in order to prepare the service user to be able to deal with them. In discussing with a practice teacher or supervisor the way we think about and plan action, it is necessary to be able to outline why we do and do not take action. Giving our reasons exposes the work to honest appraisal and scrutiny, and protects from accusations of poor professional practice at a later stage. We may think through the issues at the time almost at the speed of light and without documenting or discussing them. Exposing our thoughts and practice to internal scrutiny enables us to justify our actions in the moment and using EI is one way of doing this. Critical reflections in and on practice and a reflexive mindset all fit well with the suite of competencies in EI, and with the interpersonal skills, values and beliefs embedded in social work practice.

So you see the justification of not doing one's duty – investigating potential abuse in this case – was made on the basis of the social worker allowing the service user to deal with a crisis situation in order that the comments of the previous day could be further explored and possible action taken.

However, should the possibility of child abuse have taken priority? What if child abuse had surfaced and it was disclosed by the service user that she had told you about the possibility of this the day before? Would you think it appropriate for the social worker to visit the service user's house to verify the authenticity of the phone call, or to present a case for allowing the service user to visit with the social worker? May the whole thing have been a hoax to allow the service user some time out of therapy/with the family?

It is important not to be seduced by the crisis but to maintain a clear focus on what solutions might be. We would aim to be non-judgemental yet adaptable and innovative in integrating the service user's needs with the agency procedures and responsibilities. This leads on to the idea of synergy in practice where there is a coming together of cognitive (knowledge) skills and affective (practice) skills with a third element of emotional intelligence skills mediating in and between the other two. A social worker who has a good theoretical knowledge and who is an enthusiastic report writer but does not have emotional intelligence is unlikely to achieve optimum results for service users.

# Practice confidence, trustworthiness and conscientiousness

One of the recent developments within healthcare is that of moral insight and virtue ethics (Bolsin et al., 2005; Begley, 2006). It is argued by these authors that the practice of whistle-blowing should be aligned constructively towards self-reporting and personal development that emphasises the conscience and moral character of the practitioner as agent. Further, that practical wisdom grows from habitual practice and along with theory forms two parts of the triumvirate, the third being excellence of character. Two character attributes that are often applied to social workers are that they are trustworthy and conscientious in their work.

Goleman describes trustworthiness as being able to:

> *act ethically and above reproach, build trust through their reliability and authenticity, admit their own mistakes and confront unethical actions in others, take tough principled stands even if they are unpopular.*

(Goleman, 1998, p89)

And conscientiousness as being able to:

> *meet commitments and keep promises, hold themselves accountable for meeting their objectives, being organised and careful in their work.*

(Goleman, 1998, p90)

These character attributes sit comfortably with the values and code of conduct for social work and with elements of the National Occupational Standards. Yet in practice one is often seduced into the technical rationality of practice. This can mean seeing accountability as the completion of forms, understanding being careful as not taking risks, acting ethically as protecting colleagues from scrutiny and going with the status quo rather than upsetting the applecart.

However, if you think about your social work education you will see straight away that your bachelor or Master's degree will normally reside within the arts. That means within the sphere of creativity, lateral thinking, using innovation to root out new understandings, examining existing structures and practice, and forging questioning techniques with which to challenge the status quo. Art is never a static enterprise but constantly shifting and reinventing itself in line with new materials, global advances, different techniques and interpretations. One only has to think about the cow-pickling activities of Damian Hurst and his resultant huge fortune to realise that art is indeed a discipline where reinvention pays large dividends.

In setting ourselves up as confident, trustworthy, conscientious practitioners, we need to be creative about how we realise the impact we have on others.

---

ACTIVITY *6.7*

*A first-year student became ostracised from his group because he was always taking an oppositional stand in any debate. His peers took this to mean that he thought he was so clever that only his view mattered. Because he did not agree with them they assumed that he wanted to persuade them to come over to his side. They saw this as 'giving in' and an entrenched chasm grew between them.*

*Under the two headings of trustworthiness and conscientiousness, apply your thoughts to this case study. Keep your responses in your learning log.*

---

## Comment

You might think that having someone like this in any group is really useful because it enables alternative ideas to be considered. In a practice setting too, having someone who can think through alternatives, perhaps what the implication of actions might be, can enable us to see that our first reaction might not always be the best one. You might think he can be relied upon to give the group a thorough appraisal of situations.

You might feel that he could be helped to see that while it is useful for him to give alternative responses to the debate, he might instead prompt other group members to do this, having the effect of developing their questioning skills and not always proffering his own views.

He might also be helped to see that in not considering the views of others he is missing out on his own personal development. Most powerful practitioners often remain silent while evaluating what others say and then having processed this are more able to synthesise solutions. They are more trusted to give a balanced and well-thought-through answer.

Faced with more convincing arguments, he would be more able to accept these rather than feel he must continue to hold his own less powerful argument instead of losing face. Seeing compromise and allowing for the affirmation of others enables us to admit our mistakes as part of our professional development, rather than carrying envy or jealousy towards them.

Being organised in practice goes hand-in-hand with being organised in thinking, planning, challenging, adapting and reapplying, rather like Kolb's reflective cycle. So in contributing to a debate the cycle of reflection moves from the concrete example, say, of the debate, towards thinking through the topic and contributions, planning your own contribution and any challenge to others, listening and adapting to their response and then reapplying your own understandings to the topic. In this way organisation, accountability and conscientiousness are applied to each element of the debate in a professional way.

In this example the key is to see how the positive elements can be drawn out to enable the focus to be upon growth and understanding rather than the initial students' responses of ostracism and blame. How do you think this would apply to your development as a critical practitioner?

---

### ACTIVITY 6.8

*Here are three example scenarios of practice. Take each in turn and list your ideas about how you might demonstrate your practice confidence using the skills of being a trustworthy and conscientious practitioner. In being critical you will also be posing questions to yourself about the dilemmas and tensions that this creates for all involved.*

1. *A service user who uses drugs tells you that he has begun selling drugs in order to service his habit.*
2. *A social work colleague tells you that he is employing one of his service users who is an out-of-work carpenter because he can pay him less.*
3. *A health professional is putting pressure on you to advise an Asian mother you are working with to admit her low-weight child to hospital.*

---

### Comment

In each of these scenarios there may initially appear to be clear-cut action. In thinking through the consequences it will be come apparent that there are nuances here based on legal, ethical, cultural, class and professional considerations. Do we have a duty to inform others of the consequences of their actions, to whistle-blow or to involve the judiciary? What might be the consequences for us if we don't take that action – do we risk collusion and – by association – guilt?

Feeling uncomfortable about scenarios like these tells us that we have good ethical radar. Deciding what to do, how to do it and why we should do it creates opportunities for us to demonstrate our values and beliefs ethically. For not to do anything would leave us feeling anxious, often having physical effects and being self-disappointed.

## Striving for excellence

So far we have exposed some of the qualities of a critical practitioner for consideration and Goleman states that we cannot be expected to possess all of these but enough to create a critical mass that acts as a catalyst to our practice. This is something that, after initial qualification, keeps us fresh, drives us to have enquiring minds, causes us to deal with the less obvious and gives us the confidence of performing a job well done. Seizing the day with drive and enthusiasm, optimism and hope and setting objectives to meet with high standards are all part of Goleman's self-mastery suite. How is this possible within the contested and shifting nature of social work practice and the ever-present fear of burnout, stress and disillusionment within an environment of increasing managerialism?

The first step is to recognise that there will be elements of euphoria and despair in any profession. Your protection against this, as a critical practitioner, is that you will create an ability to bear the emotional content of the work because of the way in which you bring knowledge, experience and criticality to your practice. Part of this will be the identification and management of risk and the optimism in negotiating risk-averse, actuarial risk or risk-promotion strategies with your agency, service users and colleagues.

While working in a college of adult education I had responsibilities for the promotion of access for disabled people. Some of my teaching colleagues were very creative in giving reasons why disabled people could not join their classes. Among these were:

- other students wouldn't like it;

- it would be dangerous for the disabled person;

- a disabled student wouldn't have the prior knowledge to deal with the subject complexity;

- what would they do at break time?

- a disabled person might cut her/himself (pattern cutting);

- they wouldn't be able to read the instructions;

- I wouldn't be able to communicate with them (also vice versa);

- it would be dangerous for them if there were a fire/wouldn't hear the alarm/mobility impaired and unable to use the lift.

Through using the starting point of anti-discriminatory practice and beginning with access as a human rights-based issue it was possible to think through the reasons and implications of these comments. In this way the comments were depersonalised and could be dealt with outside of any personalities. When the reasons were analysed and understood, plans could be made for action to support service users (students) and reassure staff. This was done by challenging assumptions in a collaborative way.

- I'm sure you wouldn't want to exclude X. Shall we work together to find a way to be more inclusive?

- Shall I find out if X has any qualifications in [the discipline] already, then you will know where to begin with them?

- What stage are the other students at? Maybe X could support some of them.

- Can you tell me what the pre-requirements for your course are and then I can support X in getting them?

- X will be enrolling in the usual way; is there anything they need to know about how to go about this?

- Would you like X to tell you about her previous experience in this field?

- Maybe it would be useful for you if I arrange for a volunteer to come with X, to help with those physical activities that are difficult for X to reach.

Also underpinning this type of thinking is what Howe (2008), quoting Stern, calls intersubjectivity. This is the notion that often unspoken connections are made between people seeking co-operation, cohesion, belonging and acceptance. These connections facilitate a knowing and understanding of each other and in doing so allow a (re)defining and (re)-forming of ourselves. We each like to be liked and in feeling that our protagonist (as many people might have classed me in my role in the college) sees the potential within us, so that despite our concerns, we are more inclined to attempt some of the solutions they suggest. This is, of course, part of the persuasive art of the social worker, to express our willingness to participate in the development of others, colleagues or service users, family, friends (and not forgetting social work lecturers too). Skills in facilitating collaboration include education, mentoring, giving feedback, knowing how much to ask of another, rewarding strengths and identifying areas for development.

Of course, it goes without saying that the practice of social work does not take place in a vacuum but within a plethora of organisations, so that in using all the expertise discussed so far we need to factor in the important issue of 'context'. By that I mean a consideration of how we might experience the working environment from a highly bureaucratised agency through to one that is a flat and organic provider, and all points in between. What we know about hierarchies is that:

- managerialism tends to be top down and coal-face ideas are hard or impossible to push up the system;
- systems contain powerful individuals with multiple agendas so that often the individual need overrules the corporate need;
- the system maintains the status quo and therefore change is undesirable;
- attempts at change tend to result in some slight deviation yet retain static conditions;
- the Head rules the body of workers and is seen as having the knowledge about what is the solution to problems and a monopoly in truth knowing;
- emotions are seen as dangerous rather than creative;
- motivation is done through criticism and fear, and via division and competition.

In Chapter 5 the Multiple Intelligences (MI) approach incorporated the notion of Appreciative Inquiry (AI) and it is to these strategies that we now return in the development of the Critical Social Work Practitioner within organisations.

In their book *Appreciative Inquiry for Change Management*, Lewis et al. (2008) relate the impact of social constructionism, globalisation and the rise of information technology, the human system and the search for hope in a world of stress and anxiety, and postmodernism and the risk society. Their view is that through using the strategy of story, conversation, creativity and questioning, organisations can focus on all that is not right with the world of hierarchy and bureaucracy. One method they recommend is the use of the 'World Café'. Although this method is generally used with small groups in large organisations the theory also works well through having several individual conversations at strategic levels within organisations, just as the student did in the case example on p108–9 (in the comments section following Activity 6.1). Have a look at this website, and then use the principles in the following scenario: www.theworldcafe.com/articles/STCoverStory.pdf

*In a specialist social work service to Deaf people, service users often took time from work to visit the social worker during office hours. This was frequently to ask for clarification of received letters. The new social worker applied a rights perspective and deduced that this was unequal as it meant that they would lose pay, lose their employment or that employers would believe them to have numerous social problems.*

*As a critical practitioner, how might you apply the 5D approach of AI to organisational change to develop new service provision to deal with this inequality?*

## Comment

Taking each of the domains in order, the practitioner may have developed the following framework for organisational change. Some questions are posed indicating that using AI can be a risky enterprise if not encompassed as a whole organisation conversation.

## Define

This phase should be open-minded, exciting for stakeholders and with an eye to the potential outcomes. The questions to be explored should encourage participation. So rather than focusing on the 'problem' of Deaf people taking time from work and occupying professional's time, this could be reframed as 'the development of translation advocacy to Deaf service users in accessing written communications'. The question is of vital importance in setting the context for AI development.

## Discover

This phase begins by looking at the key strengths of what exists in the organisation and exploring the best of this. In this case, a continuing professional development session could focus on what institutional practices there are that support Deaf service users. These can be formed into 'stories' and best practice, positive feelings and enthusiasm for the work. Through small group work, decisions are made about which ideas should go forward into the next stage. In using the World Café idea all of this can be visually presented, thereby making it accessible to Deaf people and leaving an accountable bedrock for further action. It would be important to gather accurate statistics as to the scale of the issue. For example, on a monthly basis how many people sought help with interpreting legal documents, letters, invoices, etc., and how much time did they take off from work? Then some comparison with how non-Deaf people managed these affairs, for example asking friends and family, or phoning the source of the letter for clarification. It would be possible to say that Deaf people were experiencing difficulties because of who they are, e.g. disabled, rather than that they lacked the ability to understand such letters if they were presented in an appropriate medium, for example sign language or clear language. Additionally, the worker might feel that such people were taking up professional time that could usefully be used more effectively, e.g. in the education of other professionals about the needs of Deaf people in child care, mental health, older people's services, probation, adoption, housing and work, thereby improving provision globally across all services.

The question to answer is not to identify this as a problem but as a target for change in order to offer better services. This area of work is often seen as a minority concern and busy professionals would not prioritise it or see it as an issue of equality. Managers generally have little understanding of the oppressive elements experienced by Deaf service users as deafness is a hidden disability. The social worker will need considerable strength to drive this through to management in order to change provision. How do you think using the World Café idea could be embedded in the organisation using the equality debate? How would you set about organising this and what would be your rationale as to whether to involve service users in the activity?

## Dream

In consultation with service users you might involve them in your statistical analysis, share dreams for enhanced provision and use the ideas generated during the 'Discovery' phase. You might do a cost/benefit analysis. What would be the pros and cons of, say, a separate/ voluntary/evening/weekly/mentoring system that releases the professional's time and gives a confidential and accurate service to users? How might Deaf people themselves receive some development to enable them to take on these roles? Are there any staff members who would like to learn sign language or already have awards in this? How would you convince the organisation to resource this? Might Deaf people prefer to continue to use the professional worker and, if so, how will you work with them to explore how that role may be more usefully deployed to the benefit of Deaf people generally, for example as an advocate to those previously mentioned services?

The dream phase can lift people beyond day-to-day activity and look towards happier solutions, but it can also raise expectations that cannot be fulfilled in the short term. This phase is then about looking to the longer term for organisational change.

## Design/Destiny

In the final phase of AI small task groups are formed to carry the work as identified in the three previous phases. This is also a time to celebrate creativity, inspiration and co-operation. Some ideas to take forward might be:

- The identification of resourcing to recruit and train volunteer advocates.

- The provision of interpreters for Deaf people to take part in this training.

- Staff development programmes to contain integral training awareness for Deaf persons' needs.

- Promotion of all staff to learn sign language.

- A statistical group to decide how best to use the data gathered and to prepare cost/ benefit analyses for resourcing purposes to develop a broader span of service provision.

These groups would take responsibility for leading their ideas forward and occasionally report to the whole group on their progress. The outcome from each group would lead to a 'Delivery' phase where each element reached fruition. In this way the sum of the parts of AI both emanate from an holistic organisational view and feedback into it, causing it to change and evolve as having a greater fit for purpose.

# Political awareness and influence

In a sense, all of the skills used in EI and AI within your development as a critical practitioner are underpinned by a political (with a small 'p') reading of situations and of those who occupy them as agents. These could be termed the micro political elements of critical practice. A sensitivity to agency cultural practices such as who to confide in, when the best time would be to request and give support, how to recognise innovative solutions, accurately read organisational policies and the practice realities that are superimposed upon them, all lead critical practitioners to use their knowledge of the organisation and their personal and professional skills in the most effective way. However, Political (with a large 'P') acumen at a macro level is vital if critical practitioners are to maximise their impact on change.

Here are some examples where a social worker has used both political and Political knowledge to achieve maximum change for service users.

1. While working to reintegrate deaf and disabled students from an out-of-area residential school, a social worker put together a case to the housing department to create an adapted facility in a housing priority area redevelopment. She included some of her adult service users who were similarly disabled but who wanted to live independent lives. She put forward the suggestion that a signing deaf person be appointed by the housing department as a warden to oversee the adapted flats. She did this in conjunction with a local teacher of the deaf and her knowledge of the responsibility of the housing department to provide such accommodation. The scheme was implemented and not only was it without cost to the Social Services Department but she found that her workload had decreased as the warden was able to deal with many everyday matters.

2. A service for black women's mental health was constantly seeking stimulating activities for their service users. The social worker running the project noticed that the local FE college had produced a new leaflet containing a mission statement. This stated:

   *We offer a service to all local residents that prides itself on welcoming diversity, creating innovative learning environments and offering opportunities for people to gain qualifications to enhance their capacity for employment.*

   The social worker asked for an appointment to meet the principal to discuss how this statement would apply to her service users. In advance she had discussed the various courses with her service users and ascertained those that would be of interest to them. She had also agreed with her manager what support the project might be able to give to the college so that she would have a bargaining position. The college decided to run a trial basic education course on employability skills. This would be free and the college benefited because they could show this as meeting some of the government's initiatives on schemes aimed at building social capital for the long-term unemployed. The principal also thought it might be worth applying for European funds for this work. As a result, half of the group decided to join other mainstream courses in English and maths, and one person joined a 'cooking for one' programme. The benefits to the women were seen as vastly increased confidence, happier mood and improvements in appearance, taking more responsibilities in the project and increased ability in managing finances.

Although these examples were political in the sense that they were seated in local policy, having a broader political awareness is essential in the understanding of the position that most of our service users occupy as 'the other'. By that I mean that due to social policy, party politics, societal discourse and the influence of the media, those people who seek social work services are, in the main, poor, unemployed, unqualified, from minority groups, lone parents, lower class, disabled/ill or possess less influence due to their status as women, older people, refugees and asylum seekers or migrant workers. For example, asylum seekers' children are more likely to be taken into care due to recent legislation, older people are more likely to be denied access to health care because workers command priority places, lone mothers are blamed for delinquency, migrant workers experience a pull/push factor to supply cheap labour or are vilified for taking host jobs. A clear example of social workers politicising their work is where those working in child protection services join the Child Poverty Action Group (CPAG) in order to lobby government for better resourcing for lone parents. So the central argument here is that critical practitioners need to understand the forces that shape the views and actions of powerful players and realise the effect this has on those who are less powerful in order to detect crucial power networks and use these to the advantage of service users, and to accurately read their own legitimate power and that of their agencies.

In summation, Goleman identifies a raft of social skills that promote the ability to use political influence within emotional intelligence. He refers to these under the heading of 'people skills' as follows.

| | |
|---|---|
| Influence | wielding effective tactics of persuasion |
| Communication | sending clear and consistent messages |
| Conflict management | negotiating and managing disagreements |
| Leadership | inspiring and guiding |
| Change catalyst | initiating, promoting or managing change |

(Goleman, 1998, p168)

---

### ACTIVITY 6.10

*Look back at examples 1 and 2 on p129. Identify in each example how Goleman's five people-skills areas were being used. Record your responses in your learning log.*

---

## Comment

In both cases the social workers used their influence situating this in law, professional responsibilities and equality-of-opportunity policy. They took the lead in communicating questions for debate, identifying potential solutions, and in managing the meeting schedules and content. They used conflict as a focus for change with all group members taking responsibility. They had realised the potential for change and employed their leadership in driving the issues forward. With the support of their line managers, both social workers had been able to use some initial set-up resourcing to pump-prime the change.

# Are you a 'good enough practitioner' or a critical practitioner?

Finally, I want to take Butler and Hope's (2007) example of the Laming Report on the death of Victoria Climbié and to compare the good enough worker and the emotionally intelligent worker. The inquiry highlighted the failure to do the simplest things in recognising the danger to which Victoria was exposed. The social worker visited the family numerous times but was told that Victoria was sleeping, out, not available. Although one social worker reported that Victoria looked like *an advert for Action Aid* and she had not been seen for some considerable time, these turns of events did not trigger the simple reaction that action needed to be taken. The social worker was going through the motions of attempting to make contact as required under the law but was not able to give meaning to what was happening. Maybe the truth was too painful for the worker to bear, perhaps she was aware of the racial sensitivities, of her own uncertainty in taking action, of her lack of support from her manager or lack of a clear agency policy. Whatever the reason, she failed to see what became obvious in the inquiry – that the child should have been removed under the law. It is not good enough to follow the usual everyday practice of visiting, interviewing, assessing and reporting. These activities should lead use to make a plan of action for the good of the service user, their carers and families, and use our professional knowledge, skills and values in association with the emotional intelligence of critical practice. This means analysing what has happened, how it happened and why; what our responses might be and why the one we choose appears at that time to be the best possible response. In addition, you should be considering what might have been the possible outcomes of action that you chose not to take. In doing this, you are practising your skills as a critical practitioner using reflection to cognitively bank the mental processes involved in thinking and anticipating action.

---

**CHAPTER SUMMARY**

- This chapter has brought together the elements that make up critical practice and given you some examples of students who were developing as critical practitioners. Through the activities and comments it has introduced you to examples of the nuances, dilemmas and tensions that you can expect to challenge your practice. Remember at the beginning of this book we saw that social work was a contested and shifting activity and was in a sense a victim of political, social and philosophical discourses on the nature of the human experience. In this chapter it has been possible to integrate emotional intelligence as a central element to your practice and to use the attributes of EI to give you some basis for a framework of emotional practice in addition to the knowledge and theories that you will have as a qualified practitioner. Indeed, Goleman's writings tell us that these three domains must be present if we are to be consummate professionals. Overall through practice, reflection, reframing, thinking and reapplying, you will have emphasised the importance of critical reflective practice through embedding the activities within actual student practice learning examples.

*Continued*

---

**CHAPTER SUMMARY** *Continued*

- Finally, you should realise that although the activities that have led you to become more critically reflective have been completed by each reader, you have each accomplished a unique expression of this in your learning log. This is the power of critical reflection: that it enables you to reason through why you have or have not taken action. In a sense, this ability is your armour of professionalism, not to desensitise you from feelings but to give you the courage and belief in yourself in order that you can survive and flourish within the forthcoming challenges that are waiting for you.

---

**My haiku**
Skills of social work.
Challenge, courage, self-control
EI and critique.

---

**ACTIVITY 6.11**

*Try writing a critical practitioner haiku and put this in your learning log.*

---

**FURTHER READING**

**Knott, C and Scragg, T** (2007) *Reflective practice in social work.* Exeter: Learning Matters.

A text that takes you into a deeper understanding of the essential qualities of a social work practitioner. This text explores some of the more traditional attributes such as reflection, feelings and emotion in social work but also integrates some of the more contemporary applications of emotional intelligence, social capital development and habitus. The synthesis of reason, social and emotional noise with practice all come together to make this book an essential text to accompany *Critical learning for social work.*

**Thompson, S and Thompson, N** (2008) *The critically reflective practitioner.* Basingstoke: Palgrave Macmillan.

An easy-to-read text that incorporates many complex ideas in an accessible way. There are numerous examples of practitioner accounts of reflection as voiced quotes or reflective writing. Essentially this text takes you beyond the simply reflective into the realms of the critically reflective practitioner.

**USEFUL WEBSITES**

Type 'critical reasoning and social work' in the search box of your browser and go to 'scholarly articles'. This will give you a large number of different resources on critical practice and social work.

**www.iriss.org.uk**

In the search box at the top-right corner type 'critical incident analysis', then choose the article 'New Assessment Methods; evaluation of an innovative method of assessment – critical incident analysis, by Crisp, BR, Lister, PG and Dutton, K (2005) This research article makes the links between critical incident analysis used to develop social work students' ability to develop as critical practitioners.

# Conclusion

This book has taken you through a developmental process by raising your awareness of how to ask critical questions, how to read and write with a critical eye, and how to apply these skills to critical reasoning and to approaches employing multiple intelligences. Finally, you will have brought all these together to launch your career as a critical practitioner. You have used the activities contained here to practise all of these attributes and responded to, and reflected upon these, in your learning log.

Of course, this is not all there is to it. This is not the place to stop. First you will complete your practice placements on your course, then undertake your ASYE. Following your status as a registered practitioner you will continue to work through the continuing professional development framework offered through the Professional Capabilities Framework (PCF) – and finally perhaps a post-qualifying course within your discipline. What you will be doing is consistently applying your experience and theory to redefine how you practise. You may also think about how you contribute to theory making by conducting action research yourself. This constant infusion of criticality through reflection, evaluation, practice and research not only gives you the armour of professionalism but also lifts the profile of the social work profession. You are not in it alone, either for the good – plaudits when you do well – or for the bad – crisis-provoked adverse publicity. In practising critically you will be able to bear the emotional content of the work with professionalism, integrity and through the myriad lenses of ethical consideration. These are some of the things that I hope you will have gained by working through this book.

# Critical learning log

Here is a list of the critical learning activities in this book. If you proceed through these gradually you will be able to create experiences that support you to become a critical social work practitioner. Keep a separate book, loose-leaf folder or an e-journal for all your responses. To keep track of where you are up to, tick off each activity as you complete them. Remember it can be useful to work through the activities with a peer or mentor.

## Chapter 1 – Developing critical questions

Tick when completed

Activity 1.1
Your current position within critical learning.
Using the critical questions framework with your next assignment.
☐

Activity 1.2
Lone mothers.
☐

Activity 1.3
Consolidation quiz.
☐

Activity 1.4
Pose questions using the four areas of the questions framework ready for your next assignment.
☐

Activity 1.5
Getting to grips with connecting questions.
☐

Activity 1.6
Composing hypothesis questions.
☐

Activity 1.7
Critical questioning.
☐

Activity 1.8
Revisit the true/false quiz.
☐

Activity 1.9
What sort of a learner are you?
(You will need a critical friend with you for this one.)
☐

Activity 1.10
Questions to ask yourself at the end of the chapter.
☐

Activity 1.11
Creating a critical friendship.
☐

Activity 1.12
Your haiku. ☐

## Chapter 2 – Developing critical reading

Activity 2.1
Read the article 'Money troubles'. ☐

Activity 2.2 ☐
Who is the audience?
What are the main claims?
In what context is the writer making these claims?
Is the evidence convincing and how would I evaluate it?
What is the position of the author?
Are the points and arguments well developed?
Is the argument deep or surface level?
Do I agree with or refute it and why?
How would I evaluate the content?

Activity 2.3 ☐
This is a reading activity. Respond to the three questions in the three-step
guide to critical reading of the student volunteer interview.
What does the text say – what information is imparted and
what knowledge do I gain from it?
What does the text do – what concerns and implications
does it raise for me?
What does it mean – how does it stretch my thinking
about the topic?

Activity 2.4 ☐
Read the article 'Social work in Britain' and complete the 20
questions quiz. Then check your answers at the end of Chapter 2.

Activity 2.5 ☐
Annotation activity.

Activity 2.6 ☐
Critical annotation of a poem.

Activity 2.7 ☐
Annotation of websites.

Activity 2.8 ☐
Your haiku.

## Chapter 3 – Developing critical writing

Activity 3.1 ☐
Your definitions of anti-oppressive and anti-discriminatory practice.

Activity 3.2
Defining terms using academic and sophisticated writing. ☐

Activity 3.3
Where are you on the apprentice–master continuum? ☐

Activity 3.4
Using commas. ☐

Activity 3.5
Ownership and the disappearing letter. ☐

Activity 3.6
Using metaphor. ☐

Activity 3.7
Your haiku. ☐

# Chapter 4 – Developing critical reasoning

Activity 4.1
Dealing with sexism and homophobia. ☐

Activity 4.2
Premises and conclusions. ☐

Activity 4.3
Maternity ward. ☐

Activity 4.4
Redefining as premises and conclusions. ☐

Activity 4.5
Student anti-discriminatory practice. ☐

Activity 4.6
Technical rationalist or professional artist? ☐

Activity 4.7
Applying critical reasoning. ☐

Activity 4.8
Assumption and bias questions. ☐

Activity 4.9
Reading activity on assumption and bias. ☐

Activity 4.10
Mrs F and her social worker's report. ☐

Activity 4.11
Your haiku. ☐

# Chapter 5 – Developing a critical approach using multiple intelligences

Activity 5.1
Mary's case study and MI ☐

Activity 5.2
Mary's case study and EI ☐

Activity 5.3
Mary's case study and EI ☐

Activity 5.4
Applying AI and the 5 Ds ☐

# Chapter 6 – Developing as a critical practitioner

Activity 6.1
Mental health admission. ☐

Activity 6.2
Student critical event. ☐

Activity 6.3
Responding to critical incident log. ☐

Activity 6.4
Matching emotional intelligence attributes to examples. ☐

Activity 6.5
Attributes and difficulties. ☐

Activity 6.6
Substance misuse meeting and action plan. ☐

Activity 6.7
Trustworthiness and conscientiousness. ☐

Activity 6.8
Practice confidence skills. ☐

Activity 6.9
Using AI for organisational change. ☐

Activity 6.10
Using of Goleman's five people-skills areas. ☐

Activity 6.11
Your final haiku! ☐

**Congratulations!**
Well done, you are now a critical social work practitioner!

# Appendix 1 Professional capabilities framework

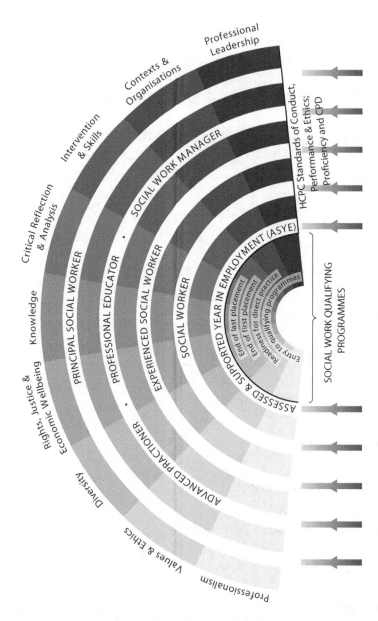

*Professional Capabilities Framework diagram reproduced with permission of The College of Social Work*

# Appendix 2    Subject benchmark for social work

## 4 Defining principles

4.1   As an applied academic subject, social work is characterised by a distinctive focus on practice in complex social situations to promote and protect individual and collective well-being. This underscores the importance of partnerships between HEIs and service providers to ensure the full involvement of practitioners, managers, tutors, service users and carers with students in both academic and practice learning and assessment.

4.2   At honours level, the study of social work involves the integrated study of subject-specific knowledge, skills and values and the critical application of research knowledge from the social and human sciences, and from social work (and closely related domains) to inform understanding and to underpin action, reflection and evaluation. Honours degree programmes should be designed to help foster this integration of contextual, analytic, critical, explanatory and practical understanding.

4.3   Contemporary definitions of social work as a degree subject reflect its origins in a range of different academic and practice traditions. The precise nature and scope of the subject is itself a matter for legitimate study and critical debate. Three main issues are relevant to this.

- Social work is located within different social welfare contexts. Within the UK there are different traditions of social welfare (influenced by legislation, historical development and social attitudes) and these have shaped both social work education and practice in community-based settings including residential, day care and substitute care. In an international context, distinctive national approaches to social welfare policy, provision and practice have greatly influenced the focus and content of social work degree programmes.

- There are competing views in society at large on the nature of social work and on its place and purpose. Social work practice and education inevitably reflect these differing perspectives on the role of social work in relation to social justice, social care and social order.

- Social work, both as occupational practice and as an academic subject, evolves, adapts and changes in response to the social, political and economic challenges and demands of contemporary social welfare policy, practice and legislation.

4.4   Honours graduates in social work should therefore be equipped both to understand, and to work within, this context of contested debate about nature, scope and purpose, and be enabled to analyse, adapt to, manage and eventually to lead the processes of change.

4.5   The applied nature of social work as an academic subject means that practice is an essential and core element of learning. The following points clarify the use of the term 'practice' in the statement.

- The term 'practice' in this statement is used to encompass learning that not only takes place in professional practice placements, but also in a variety of other experiential learning situations. All learning opportunities that bear academic credit must be subject to methods of assessment appropriate to their academic level and be assessed by competent assessors. Where they form part of the curriculum leading to integrated academic and professional awards, practice learning opportunities will also be subject to regulations that further define learning requirements, standards and modes of assessment.

- In honours degree programmes covered by this statement, practice as an activity refers to experiential, action-based learning. In this sense, practice provides opportunities for students to improve and demonstrate their understanding and competence through the application and testing of knowledge and skills.

- Practice activity is also a source of transferable learning in its own right. Such learning can transfer both from a practice setting to the 'classroom' and vice versa. Thus practice can be as much a source of intellectual and cognitive learning as other modes of study. For this reason, learning through practice attracts full academic credit.

- Learning in practice can include activities such as observation, shadowing, analysis and research, as well as intervention within social work and related organisations. Practice learning on honours degrees involves active engagement with service users and others in practice settings outside the university and may involve, for example, virtual/simulated practice, observational and research activities.

4.6   Social work is a moral activity that requires practitioners to recognise the dignity of the individual, but also to make and implement difficult decisions (including restriction of liberty) in human situations that involve the potential for benefit or harm. Honours degree programmes in social work therefore involve the study, application of, and critical reflection upon, ethical principles and dilemmas. As reflected by the four care councils' codes of practice, this involves showing respect for persons, honouring the diverse and distinctive organisations and communities that make up contemporary society, promoting social justice and combating processes that lead to discrimination, marginalisation and social exclusion. This means that honours undergraduates must learn to:

- recognise and work with the powerful links between intrapersonal and interpersonal factors and the wider social, legal, economic, political and cultural context of people's lives

- understand the impact of injustice, social inequalities and oppressive social relations

- challenge constructively individual, institutional and structural discrimination

- practise in ways that maximise safety and effectiveness in situations of uncertainty and incomplete information

- help people to gain, regain or maintain control of their own affairs, insofar as this is compatible with their own or others' safety, well-being and rights

- work in partnership with service users and carers and other professionals to foster dignity, choice and independence, and effect change.

4.7   The expectation that social workers will be able to act effectively in such complex circumstances requires that honours degree programmes in social work should be designed to help students learn to become accountable, reflective, critical and evaluative. This involves learning to:

- think critically about the complex social, legal, economic, political and cultural contexts in which social work practice is located

- work in a transparent and responsible way, balancing autonomy with complex, multiple and sometimes contradictory accountabilities (for example, to different service users, employing agencies, professional bodies and the wider society)

- exercise authority within complex frameworks of accountability and ethical and legal boundaries

- acquire and apply the habits of critical reflection, self-evaluation and consultation, and make appropriate use of research in decision-making about practice and in the evaluation of outcomes.

# 5 Subject knowledge, understanding and skills

## Subject knowledge and understanding

5.1   During their degree studies in social work, honours graduates should acquire, critically evaluate, apply and integrate knowledge and understanding in the following five core areas of study.

5.1.1   **Social work services, service users and carers**, which include:

- the social processes (associated with, for example, poverty, migration, unemployment, poor health, disablement, lack of education and other sources of disadvantage) that lead to marginalisation, isolation and exclusion, and their impact on the demand for social work services

- explanations of the links between definitional processes contributing to social differences (for example, social class, gender, ethnic differences, age, sexuality and religious belief) to the problems of inequality and differential need faced by service users

- the nature of social work services in a diverse society (with particular reference to concepts such as prejudice, interpersonal, institutional and structural discrimination, empowerment and anti-discriminatory practices)

- the nature and validity of different definitions of, and explanations for, the characteristics and circumstances of service users and the services required by them, drawing on knowledge from research, practice experience, and from service users and carers

- the focus on outcomes, such as promoting the well-being of young people and their families, and promoting dignity, choice and independence for adults receiving services

- the relationship between agency policies, legal requirements and professional boundaries in shaping the nature of services provided in interdisciplinary contexts and the issues associated with working across professional boundaries and within different disciplinary groups.

5.1.2 **The service delivery context**, which includes:

- the location of contemporary social work within historical, comparative and global perspectives, including European and international contexts

- the changing demography and cultures of communities in which social workers will be practising

- the complex relationships between public, social and political philosophies, policies and priorities and the organisation and practice of social work, including the contested nature of these

- the issues and trends in modern public and social policy and their relationship to contemporary practice and service delivery in social work

- the significance of legislative and legal frameworks and service delivery standards (including the nature of legal authority, the application of legislation in practice, statutory accountability and tensions between statute, policy and practice)

- the current range and appropriateness of statutory, voluntary and private agencies providing community-based, day-care, residential and other services and the organisational systems inherent within these

- the significance of interrelationships with other related services, including housing, health, income maintenance and criminal justice (where not an integral social service)

- the contribution of different approaches to management, leadership and quality in public and independent human services

- the development of personalised services, individual budgets and direct payments

- the implications of modern information and communications technology (ICT) for both the provision and receipt of services.

5.1.3 **Values and ethics**, which include:

- the nature, historical evolution and application of social work values

- the moral concepts of rights, responsibility, freedom, authority and power inherent in the practice of social workers as moral and statutory agents

- the complex relationships between justice, care and control in social welfare and the practical and ethical implications of these, including roles as statutory agents and in upholding the law in respect of discrimination

- aspects of philosophical ethics relevant to the understanding and resolution of value dilemmas and conflicts in both interpersonal and professional contexts

- the conceptual links between codes defining ethical practice, the regulation of professional conduct and the management of potential conflicts generated by the codes held by different professional groups.

5.1.4 **Social work theory**, which includes:

- research-based concepts and critical explanations from social work theory and other disciplines that contribute to the knowledge base of social work, including their distinctive epistemological status and application to practice

- the relevance of sociological perspectives to understanding societal and structural influences on human behaviour at individual, group and community levels

- the relevance of psychological, physical and physiological perspectives to understanding personal and social development and functioning

- social science theories explaining group and organisational behaviour, adaptation and change

- models and methods of assessment, including factors underpinning the selection and testing of relevant information, the nature of professional judgement and the processes of risk assessment and decision-making

- approaches and methods of intervention in a range of settings, including factors guiding the choice and evaluation of these

- user-led perspectives

- knowledge and critical appraisal of relevant social research and evaluation methodologies, and the evidence base for social work.

5.1.5 **The nature of social work practice**, which includes:

- the characteristics of practice in a range of community-based and organisational settings within statutory, voluntary and private sectors, and the factors influencing changes and developments in practice within these contexts

- the nature and characteristics of skills associated with effective practice, both direct and indirect, with a range of service-users and in a variety of settings

- the processes that facilitate and support service user choice and independence

- the factors and processes that facilitate effective interdisciplinary, interprofessional and interagency collaboration and partnership

- the place of theoretical perspectives and evidence from international research in assessment and decision-making processes in social work practice

- the integration of theoretical perspectives and evidence from international research into the design and implementation of effective social work intervention, with a wide range of service users, carers and others

- the processes of reflection and evaluation, including familiarity with the range of approaches for evaluating service and welfare outcomes, and their significance for the development of practice and the practitioner.

## Subject-specific skills and other skills

5.2   As an applied subject at honours degree level, social work necessarily involves the development of skills that may be of value in many situations (for example, analytical thinking, building relationships, working as a member of an organisation, intervention, evaluation and reflection). Some of these skills are specific to social work but many are also widely transferable. What helps to define the specific nature of these skills in a social work context are:

- the context in which they are applied and assessed (e.g., communication skills in practice with people with sensory impairments or assessment skills in an interprofessional setting)

- the relative weighting given to such skills within social work practice (e.g., the central importance of problem-solving skills within complex human situations)

- the specific purpose of skill development (e.g., the acquisition of research skills in order to build a repertoire of research-based practice)

- a requirement to integrate a range of skills (i.e., not simply to demonstrate these in an isolated and incremental manner).

5.3   All social work honours graduates should show the ability to reflect on and learn from the exercise of their skills. They should understand the significance of the concepts of continuing professional development and lifelong learning, and accept responsibility for their own continuing development.

5.4   Social work honours graduates should acquire and integrate skills in the following five core areas.

## Problem-solving skills

5.5   These are subdivided into four areas.

5.5.1   **Managing problem-solving activities**: honours graduates in social work should be able to plan problem-solving activities, i.e. to:

- think logically, systematically, critically and reflectively

- apply ethical principles and practices critically in planning problem-solving activities

- plan a sequence of actions to achieve specified objectives, making use of research, theory and other forms of evidence

- manage processes of change, drawing on research, theory and other forms of evidence.

5.5.2 **Gathering information**: honours graduates in social work should be able to:

- gather information from a wide range of sources and by a variety of methods, for a range of purposes. These methods should include electronic searches, reviews of relevant literature, policy and procedures, face-to-face interviews, written and telephone contact with individuals and groups

- take into account differences of viewpoint in gathering information and critically assess the reliability and relevance of the information gathered

- assimilate and disseminate relevant information in reports and case records.

5.5.3 **Analysis and synthesis**: honours graduates in social work should be able to analyse and synthesise knowledge gathered for problem-solving purposes, i.e. to:

- assess human situations, taking into account a variety of factors (including the views of participants, theoretical concepts, research evidence, legislation and organisational policies and procedures)

- analyse information gathered, weighing competing evidence and modifying their viewpoint in light of new information, then relate this information to a particular task, situation or problem

- consider specific factors relevant to social work practice (such as risk, rights, cultural differences and linguistic sensitivities, responsibilities to protect vulnerable individuals and legal obligations)

- assess the merits of contrasting theories, explanations, research, policies and procedures

- synthesise knowledge and sustain reasoned argument

- employ a critical understanding of human agency at the macro (societal), mezzo (organisational and community) and micro (inter- and intrapersonal) levels

- critically analyse and take account of the impact of inequality and discrimination in work with people in particular contexts and problem situations.

5.5.4 **Intervention and evaluation**: honours graduates in social work should be able to use their knowledge of a range of interventions and evaluation processes selectively to:

- build and sustain purposeful relationships with people and organisations in community-based, and interprofessional contexts

- make decisions, set goals and construct specific plans to achieve these, taking into account relevant factors including ethical guidelines

- negotiate goals and plans with others, analysing and addressing in a creative manner human, organisational and structural impediments to change

- implement plans through a variety of systematic processes that include working in partnership

- undertake practice in a manner that promotes the well-being and protects the safety of all parties

- engage effectively in conflict resolution

- support service users to take decisions and access services, with the social worker as navigator, advocate and supporter

- manage the complex dynamics of dependency and, in some settings, provide direct care and personal support in everyday living situations

- meet deadlines and comply with external definitions of a task

- plan, implement and critically review processes and outcomes

- bring work to an effective conclusion, taking into account the implications for all involved

- monitor situations, review processes and evaluate outcomes

- use and evaluate methods of intervention critically and reflectively.

## Communication skills

5.6   Honours graduates in social work should be able to communicate clearly, accurately and precisely (in an appropriate medium) with individuals and groups in a range of formal and informal situations, i.e. to:

- make effective contact with individuals and organisations for a range of objectives, by verbal, paper-based and electronic means

- clarify and negotiate the purpose of such contacts and the boundaries of their involvement

- listen actively to others, engage appropriately with the life experiences of service users, understand accurately their viewpoint and overcome personal prejudices to respond appropriately to a range of complex personal and interpersonal situations

- use both verbal and non-verbal cues to guide interpretation

- identify and use opportunities for purposeful and supportive communication with service users within their everyday living situations

- follow and develop an argument and evaluate the viewpoints of, and evidence presented by, others

- write accurately and clearly in styles adapted to the audience, purpose and context of the communication

- use advocacy skills to promote others' rights, interests and needs

- present conclusions verbally and on paper, in a structured form, appropriate to the audience for which these have been prepared

- make effective preparation for, and lead meetings in a productive way

- communicate effectively across potential barriers resulting from differences (for example, in culture, language and age).

# Skills in working with others

5.7   Honours graduates in social work should be able to work effectively with others, i.e. to:

- involve users of social work services in ways that increase their resources, capacity and power to influence factors affecting their lives

- consult actively with others, including service users and carers, who hold relevant information or expertise

- act cooperatively with others, liaising and negotiating across differences such as organisational and professional boundaries and differences of identity or language

- develop effective helping relationships and partnerships with other individuals, groups and organisations that facilitate change

- act with others to increase social justice by identifying and responding to prejudice, institutional discrimination and structural inequality

- act within a framework of multiple accountability (for example, to agencies, the public, service users, carers and others)

- challenge others when necessary, in ways that are most likely to produce positive outcomes.

# Skills in personal and professional development

5.8   Honours graduates in social work should be able to:

- advance their own learning and understanding with a degree of independence

- reflect on and modify their behaviour in the light of experience

- identify and keep under review their own personal and professional boundaries

- manage uncertainty, change and stress in work situations

- handle inter- and intrapersonal conflict constructively

- understand and manage changing situations and respond in a flexible manner

- challenge unacceptable practices in a responsible manner

- take responsibility for their own further and continuing acquisition and use of knowledge and skills

- use research critically and effectively to sustain and develop their practice.

# ICT and numerical skills

5.9   Honours graduates in social work should be able to use ICT methods and techniques to support their learning and their practice. In particular, they should demonstrate the ability to:

- use ICT effectively for professional communication, data storage and retrieval, and information searching

- use ICT in working with people who use services

- demonstrate sufficient familiarity with statistical techniques to enable effective use of research in practice

- integrate appropriate use of ICT to enhance skills in problem-solving in the four areas set out in paragraph 6.2

- apply numerical skills to financial and budgetary responsibilities

- have a critical understanding of the social impact of ICT, including an awareness of the impact of the 'digital divide'.

# 6 Teaching, learning and assessment

6.1   At honours degree level, social work programmes explicitly recognise and maximise the use of students' prior learning and experience. Acquisition and development of the required knowledge and skills, capable of transfer to new situations and of further enhancement, mark important staging posts in the process of lifelong learning. Social work models of learning are characteristically developmental and incremental (i.e., students are expected to assume increasing responsibility for identifying their own learning needs and making use of available resources for learning). The context of learning should take account of the impact of the Bologna Process and transnational learning. The overall aims and expected final outcomes of the honours degree, together with the specific requirements of particular topics, modules or practice experiences, should inform the choice of both learning and teaching strategies and aligned formative and summative assessment methods.

6.2   The learning processes in social work at honours degree level can be expressed in terms of four interrelated themes.

- **Awareness raising, skills and knowledge acquisition** – a process in which the student becomes more aware of aspects of knowledge and expertise, learns how to systematically engage with and acquire new areas of knowledge, recognises their potential and becomes motivated to engage in new ways of thinking and acting.

- **Conceptual understanding** – a process in which a student acquires, examines critically and deepens understanding (measured and tested against existing knowledge and adjustments made in attitudes and goals).

- **Practice skills and experience** – processes in which a student learns practice skills in the contexts identified in paragraph 4.4 and applies theoretical models and research evidence together with new understanding to relevant activities, and receives feedback from various sources on performance, enhancing openness to critical self-evaluation.

- **Reflection on performance** – a process in which a student reflects critically and evaluatively on past experience, recent performance and feedback, and applies this information to the process of integrating awareness (including awareness of the impact of self on others) and new understanding, leading to improved performance.

6.3   Honours degree programmes in social work acknowledge that students learn at different rates and in diverse ways, and learn best when there is consistent and timely guidance and a variety of learning opportunities. Programmes should provide clear and accessible information about learning approaches, methods and outcomes that enable students to engage with diverse learning and teaching methods in learning settings across academic and practice environments.

6.4   Approaches to support blended learning should include the use of ICT to access data, literature and resources, as well as engagement with technologies to support communication and reflection, and sharing of learning across academic and practice learning settings.

6.5   Learning methods may include:

- learner-focused approaches that encourage active participation and staged, progressive learning throughout the degree

- the establishment of initial learning needs and the formulation of learning plans

- the development of learning networks, enabling students to learn from each other

- the involvement of practitioners and service user and carer educators.

6.6   Students should engage in a broad range of activities, including with other professionals and with service users and carers, to facilitate critical reflection. These include reading, self-directed study, research, a variety of forms of writing, lectures, discussion, seminars/tutorials, individual and group work, role plays, presentations, projects, simulations and practice experience.

6.7   Assessment strategies should show alignment between, and relevance to, social work practice, theory and assessment tasks. They should also be matched with learning outcomes and learning and teaching methods. The purpose of assessment is to:

- provide a means whereby students receive feedback regularly on their achievement and development needs

- provide tasks that promote learning, and develop and test cognitive skills, drawing on a range of sources, including the contexts of practice

- promote self-evaluation, and appraisal of their progress and learning strategies

- enable judgements to be made in relation to progress and to ensure fitness for practice, and the award, in line with professional standards.

6.8   Assessment strategies should be chosen to enhance students' abilities to conceptualise, compare and analyse issues, in order to be able to apply this in making professional judgements.

6.9   Assessment methods normally include case-based assessments, presentations and analyses, practice-focused assignments, essays, project reports, role plays/simulations, e-assessment and examinations. The requirements of honours degree programmes in social work frequently include an extended piece of written work, which may be practice-based, and is typically undertaken in the final year. This may involve independent study for either a dissertation or a project, based upon systematic enquiry and investigation. However, the requirements of research governance may restrict opportunities available to students for research involving human subjects. Where practice competences have to be assessed, as identified through national occupational standards or equivalent, opportunities should be provided for demonstration of these, together with systematic means of development, support and assessment. Assessment methods may include those listed above, in addition to observed practice, reflective logs and interview records.

6.10  Honours degree programmes in social work assess practice not as a series of discrete practical tasks, but as an integration of skills and knowledge with relevant conceptual understanding. This assessment should, therefore, contain elements that test students' critical and analytical reflective analysis. As the honours degree is an integrated academic and professional award, the failure of any core element, including assessed practice, will mean failure of the programme.

# 7 Benchmark standards

7.1  Given the essentially applied nature of social work and the co-terminosity of the degree and the professional award, students must demonstrate that they have met the standards specified in relation to both academic and practice capabilities. These standards relate to subject-specific knowledge, understanding and skills (including key skills inherent in the concept of 'graduateness'). Qualifying students will be expected to meet each of these standards in accordance with the specific standards set by the relevant country (see section 2).

## Typical graduate

7.2  Levels of attainment will vary along a continuum from the threshold to excellence. This level represents that of typical students graduating with an honours degree in social work.

## Knowledge and understanding

7.3  On graduating with an honours degree in social work, students should be able to demonstrate:

- a sound understanding of the five core areas of knowledge and understanding relevant to social work, as detailed in paragraph 5.1, including their application to practice and service delivery

- an ability to use this knowledge and understanding in an integrated way, in specific practice contexts

- an ability to use this knowledge and understanding to engage in effective relationships with service users and carers

- appraisal of previous learning and experience and ability to incorporate this into their future learning and practice

- acknowledgement and understanding of the potential and limitations of social work as a practice-based discipline to effect individual and social change

- an ability to use research and enquiry techniques with reflective awareness, to collect, analyse and interpret relevant information

- a developed capacity for the critical evaluation of knowledge and evidence from a range of sources.

## Subject-specific and other skills

7.4   On graduating with an honours degree in social work, students should be able to demonstrate a developed capacity to:

- apply creatively a repertoire of core skills as detailed in section 5

- communicate effectively with service users and carers, and with other professionals

- integrate clear understanding of ethical issues and codes of values, and practice with their interventions in specific situations

- consistently exercise an appropriate level of autonomy and initiative in individual decision-making within the context of supervisory, collaborative, ethical and organisational requirements

- demonstrate habits of critical reflection on their performance and take responsibility for modifying action in light of this.

# Glossary

**Affective domain** To do with emotion, judgement, character and conscience. Those skills that involve awareness, differentiation and integration and are associated with feelings and the ability to synthesise learning.

**Affirmation** Giving or receiving agreement, or persuading another that they are favoured.

**Anti-discriminatory** Practice that seeks to recognise and counter the making of unjust distinctions and selections for giving out unfavourable treatment often practised by the more powerful against the less powerful. Numerous acts of discrimination over time lead to oppressive practice.

**Annotation** The act of adding notes to a text to aid your own understanding or to prompt further research.

**Anti-oppressive** Practice that seeks to recognise and counter the experience of injustice brought about by being kept in subservience by the coercion of those more powerful.

**Argument** One or more premises given in support of a conclusion.

**Aspirational learning** Having a view about your own motivation, responsibility, drive, determination and confidence to believe that you will achieve. Knowing that you will never cease learning and that you need to develop strategies for transforming and enhancing your current position. This technique is also useful in working with service users who have low self-esteem.

**Axiomatic** Something that is taken for granted in, say, an argument, or a discourse or a case you are working with. For example, the claim that in debates about lone parenting, mothers are more commonly blamed for delinquency in their children, then the text would read *It is axiomatic that mothers are seen to be responsible for delinquency in their children*.

**Bed-blocking** The way older and disabled people have to prolong their stay in hospital while waiting for social care arrangements to be put in place ready for their discharge.

**Cliché** Overused, worn-out, tacky phrases often making you cringe. They waste words in assignments because they never lead the argument forward or add anything of interest to the text.

**Cognitive ability** See **Cognitive domain**.

**Cognitive domain** To do with fact, knowledge, understanding and application. Those skills that involve describing, comparing and contrasting, and are associated with abilities of the mind.

**Coherence** Having a logical flow of ideas that link themes in a meaningful way.

**Commissioning services** The act of buying services for service users following a process of assessment, brokerage and evaluation. This process may involve putting out a service specification for tendering, securing individual or block purchases and considering added value. This process can be carried out by agency commissioners, care managers or devolved to individual social workers.

**Complicity** Using words and phrases that assume we all agree with the writer.

**Consistency** Describes a situation where the focus remains constant and does not go off at a tangent.

**Context** The circumstances under which the text was written or an event has happened.

**Critical learning** Learning that integrates knowledge, analysis, synthesis and the ability to reframe ideas and debate, values and beliefs in order to challenge existing views. In social work the term can be usefully applied to an understanding of social constructionism, and how political, social and economic factors impact on individual and cultural experiences.

**Critical practice** Practice that goes beyond the functional requirements of social work to include a wider understanding of the social construction of public and personal problems. This may also include a critique of policy, discourse analysis, practice that is anti-discriminatory and anti-oppressive, and a commitment to working professionally to achieve as good an outcome as possible.

**Critical sources** These are texts (or erudite individuals) that are considered to be authoritative within your discipline area.

**Corollary** A statement that is easily proved by reference to another.

**Deductive reasoning** Drawing one conclusion by considering many positions.

**Discourse** Consists of similar thoughts and ideas on a topic. In social work terms, the discourse may be beneficial as in the case of the protection of children; or detrimental as in the vilification of sex workers.

**Economic rationality** Used in this text, it embraces the idea of supporting people to return to work and therefore relinquish income maintenance and having the benefit of paying into the country's tax system rather than drawing benefits from it. It is therefore seen as economically rational to reassess the long-term unemployed and disabled people in order that they contribute to the capitalist system rather than extract from it. These actions are often framed in a facilitative discourse by government yet felt as punitive by those they affect.

**Emancipatory paradigm** Being transformational in that any representation of views stems from those who are disadvantaged rather than by powerful structures that discriminate against them. The emancipatory strategy, research or discourse would therefore seat the views and experiences of these people above those of the funders, medical personnel or social workers carrying out the research.

**Emotional confusion** Feeling paralysed in thinking and acting because you are unable to evaluate a clear outcome. This can happen when the care and control agendas of social work seem unyielding to analysis.

**Emotional intelligence** More than academic theory, knowledge and experience, EI is the capacity for recognising ourselves as 'agents' in understanding the constant interplay with others, with our own motivational activities, and in mediation and advocacy in the promotion of effective action.

**Excavation of argument** The ways one can either support or refute arguments. This method involves the marshalling of premises, evidence, statements and assertions to promote or deny an argument. An example would be refuting the argument for the right to life as against the right to choose an abortion on the basis that the first is based on a discourse that is hugely influenced by money from the Catholic Church. The process involves digging into the reasons for the many protests supporting the right to life.

**Exemplar** An example that is considered to be an excellent guide to others. A very insightful reflective practice narrative, as included in this book, would act as an exemplar to those reading it.

**Fact** The truth backed by evidence that something has happened or will happen or a statistic demonstrated by evidence.

**Fit for purpose** Suitable for the work. This term can mean that something or someone is only meeting a minimal sufficiency in their work, rather like good-enough parenting.

**Future basing** Using a system to think yourself forward and imagine your changed situation. This might be used to plan your personal or professional development or to deal with organisational change. It is often a management tool but is also useful in practice in helping service users to transform their situations.

**Globalisation** In social work the concept that exclusion, human rights and oppression are involved in aspects of social policy and political values that shift over time depending on world movements. Examples would be the rights of women, immigration, affirmative action, the People First movement.

**Habitus** The French philosopher Pierre Bourdieu applied this term to the social sphere to mean all a person's dispositions, habits, tastes, values and beliefs as they navigate their way through the objectivity of formal life and rules, and the subjectivity of making judgements and choices. In doing this the essential qualities of the individual are influenced by their socialisation and experiences in a way that becomes cyclical in the making of those essential qualities. So by acting in certain ways under the influence of who we are, the essence of who we are changes through that experience.

**Hegemony** The way in which powerful groups maintain their power over those less powerful. This can refer to nations, e.g. Britain during the time of its former colonies, or organisations, e.g. the police and judiciary.

**Helicopter view** One of the de Bono tools that encourages you to rise above current disarray and confusion to see the whole picture. This is a useful way of making order out of chaos and can be represented by visual means.

**Hidden agenda** An ulterior motive behind some action.

**Hypothesis/hypothetical** A tentative explanation for something.

**Inductive reasoning** Taking one idea and expanding it to consider all the implications.

**Intersubjectivity** The idea that there are tacit agreements and consensus between people; people having the same professional status, experiences, class position, for example. An understanding of intersubjectivity may help in using persuasion in the light of conflict, in advocating for an oppressed person or group and in establishing improved working relationships between professionals.

**Logic** Distinguishing between good and bad reasoning used to form a view or conclusion about something.

**Jargon** Language having particular and discrete meaning for professionals that can act to exclude those not in that profession. Educational, medical, philosophical and social work language can sometimes unintentionally do this.

**Juxtapose** Provide two or more opposing or different positions from which to make your case. This causes you to look at the strengths and weakness of an issue but also to imagine alternatives.

**Medical model** A discourse instigating thinking that focuses on medical aspects of people's lives. People are seen as a collection of their symptoms to be cured and when this is not possible the system is unable to support them further than their diagnosis.

**Meta-cognition** Planning, maintaining and evaluating the self in action. Understanding how you think and working on this to improve.

**Metaphor** Using words imaginatively rather than literally to apply to ideas. For example, your learning journey where you use the idea of going from one island to another. Some may express their progress as in a speedboat reaching the other island quickly while others are using a row boat, have lost the oars and hit fog and rocks.

**Mission statement** Usually a brief statement of intent that encompasses the intention of an organisation to provide its services in a certain way to certain types of people. Generally, these statements appear to be hearts and flowers promising an all-inclusive and overarching service to users without stating that there may be a charging policy or eligibility criteria.

**Multiprofessional** Involving professionals from several different disciplines. A school may use such an approach by employing teachers, health visitors, social workers and educational psychologists.

**Not-for-profit** Outside the statutory sector of service provision. The term can mean a charitable organisation or one that covers its outgoings without intending to make a surplus profit.

**Opinion** A view of something based on personal judgement.

**Oppositional binary** Ways of thinking that give voice to the situation and experience of the less powerful. These challenge the taken-for-granted consensus view of the powerful as contentious and needing revision in favour of the oppressed.

**Premise** The supporting claim (statement) in an argument.

**Political correctness** A term used to indicate an awareness of how disadvantage is promulgated by those with power and a determination to change the assumed natural order through challenge on political grounds that recognises oppressive histories and experiences. Although of sound roots, the term PC is often used pejoratively to derail activist intentions and actions.

**Portfolio** A collection of tangible artefacts for a focused purpose. In social work this term is often applied to written contributions kept in a file for professional education and training purposes. Increasingly e-portfolios are replacing paper copies. The inclusion of practice reflections, learning experiences, recordings of influential interviews, visual representations of learning and eureka moments give depth to the portfolio.

**Problematise** To become more critical in how you think about an issue. Note that the use of this word in social work does not mean to make something a problem but to interrogate it so that you understand all its nuances and implications.

**Professional artistry** The opposite of **technical rationalism**. Using reflective and reflexive practice, feelings, imagination, intuition, critical thinking and reasoning to practise, evaluate, analyse and make judgements. Having consideration for all the human elements that are involved in working within the caring professions and that are uncontrollable, shifting and subject to interpretation.

**Protagonist** One who is the leading proponent of a cause being the central orator.

**Reasoning** Logical thinking in order to get results or reach a conclusion.

**Reflective practice** Generally, a retrospective activity where one thinks about some experience with a view to gaining deeper understanding resulting in improved practice. Social work students are often asked to write a critique to expose dilemmas and tensions in their practice. Schön describes reflection as being both on action and in action, the first being retrospective and the second during the event.

**Reflexive practice** Simply the act of delaying the immediate reaction to an event in order to think through the implications. At a deeper level the notion that in thinking through we reform our values and beliefs about an issue and that this in turn goes on to influence our practice. Some social work writers believe that reflective practice can also do this if taken to deeper levels.

**Rhetoric** Persuasive techniques used to convince the reader, often sounding pompous.

**Simile** Comparing one thing with another, e.g. 'as slippery as an eel'.

**Stakeholders** Those with an interest in the social work field. They can be social workers, employers, social care workers, service users and their carers. Peripheral stakeholders would be healthcare professionals, the media, the judiciary, elected members of council.

**Social capital** The idea that people have status, acceptance within communities, that their life experiences are validated and that they have some power and agency to effect changes in their lives.

**Social construction** Normally the idea that what we assume are givens in any society are actually constructed by powerful opinion-makers and are subject to change over time. Some ideas might be about the social construction of childhood, ageing and immigration, in fashion architecture and the setting of spurious rules of prior requirements in educational courses.

**Social model** A discourse focusing on the physical, social and attitudinal barriers that exist for people who experience ill health, disability and disadvantage. This may mean the artificial creation of physical barriers to access or the assumption about people's intellect, capabilities and possibilities. Some examples include the right of disabled people to have children, who may also be disabled, the siting of polling stations in rooms with steps or narrow doors and corridors, the creation of uneven floor surfaces.

**Stereotype** An oversimplified view of one or a group held by another or group of others.

**Strategic learning** The ability to use both deep and surface-level learning to best effect, so you may skim-read some texts yet focus on the minutiae of others.

**Structure** The flow of an article which sets the intention, leads the discussion logically and ends with a coherent conclusion.

**Subjective** Stemming from an individual perception that may include both conscious and unconscious interpretations. Not seen as scientifically unbiased but open to the 'social noise' of the human interpreter.

**Technical rationalism** The idea that theoretical applications result in certainty, prediction and control. Such an idea is manifested in managerialism in social work. The notion that if work is made the subject of functional management such as form-filling and tick-list assessment, for example, that associated with a risk analysis, the outcome will be predictable. The opposite of **professional artistry**.

**Transformational social work** That which stimulates a radical change in understanding and practice with application to social work. Often this is achieved through eureka moments where concepts such as discourse analysis, social constructionism and the mechanisms for the development of social capital are realised. It may also be realised at a lower level where the synthesis between theory, practice and knowledge-making come to be understood.

**Validity** A description of work that is sound and defensible.

**Virtuous social work** Practising in the best possible way because to do otherwise would leave you feeling uncomfortable and unprofessional, regardless of whether you are under scrutiny.

# References

Begley, A (2006) Facilitating the development of moral insight in practice: Teaching ethics and teaching virtue. *Nursing Philosophy*, 7 (4), 257–65.

Bolsin, S, Faunce, T and Oakly, J (2005) Practical virtue ethics: Healthcare whistle blowing and portable digital technology. *Journal of Medical Ethics*, 31 (10), 612–18.

Bowell, T and Kemp, G (2005) *Critical thinking: A concise guide*. 2nd edition. Oxford: Routledge.

Butler, G and Hope, T (2007) *Manage your mind*. In C Knott and T Scragg (eds) *Reflective practice in social work*. Exeter: Learning Matters.

Buzan, T (2006) *Use your head*. London: BBC Active.

Clarke, N (2006) Workplace learning in UK hospices. In S Sambrooke and J Stewart (eds) *HRD in health and social care*. London: Routledge.

Cooperrider, DL and Whitney, D (2005) *Appreciative Inquiry: A positive revolution in change*. San Francisco, CA: Berrett-Koehler.

Cottrell, S (2005) *Critical thinking skills*. Basingstoke: Palgrave Macmillan.

Dalrymple, J and Burke, B (1995) *Anti-oppressive practice: Social care and the law*. Buckingham and Philadelphia: Open University Press.

Department of Health (1996) *Community Care (Direct Payments) Act*. London: HMSO.

Dominelli, L (2002) Anti-oppressive practice in context. In R Adams, L Dominelli and M Payne (eds) *Social work themes, issues and critical debates*. Basingstoke: Palgrave Macmillan.

Entwistle, N and Ramsden, P (1983) *Understanding student learning*. London: Croom Helm.

Eysenck, MW (2000) A cognitive approach to trait anxiety. *European Journal of Personality*, 14 (5), 463–76. (Wiley Online Library. www.onlinelibrary.wiley.com. journal/10.1002/(ISSN) 1099-0984).

Fook, J (2002) *Social work: Critical theory and practice*. London: Sage.

Fook, J and Askeland, GA (2007) Challenges of critical reflection: Nothing ventured nothing gained. *Social Work Education*, 26 (5), 520–33.

Gardner, H (1993) *Multiple intelligences*. New York: Basic Books.

Gardner, H (1999) *Intelligence reframed*. New York: Basic Books.

Goleman, D (1998) *Working with emotional intelligence*. London: Bloomsbury.

Heikkila, A and Lonka, K (2006) Studies in higher education: Students' approaches to learning, self-regulation, and cognitive strategies. *Studies in Higher Education*, (31) 1, 99–117. London: Routledge.

Howe, D (2008) *The emotionally intelligent social worker*. Basingstoke: Palgrave Macmillan.

Jones, K, Cooper, B and Ferguson, H (2007) *Best practice in social work: Critical perspectives*. London: Palgrave Macmillan.

Kline, R and Preston-Shoot, M (2012) *Professional accountability in social care and health*. London: Sage/Learning Matters.

Knott, C and Scragg, T (2007) *Reflective practice in social work*. Exeter: Learning Matters.

Kolb, DA and Fry, R (1974) *Towards an applied theory of experiential learning*. Cambridge, MA: Massachusetts Institute of Technology.

Lewis, S, Passmore, J and Cantore, S (2008) *Appreciative inquiry for change management.* London: Kogan Page.

Locke, E A (2005) Why emotional intelligence is an invalid concept. *Journal of Organizational Behavior*, 26 (4), 425–31. (Wiley Online Library. www.onlinelibrary.wiley.com.journal/10.1002/(ISSN) 1099-0984).

Lymbery, M and Postle, K (2007) *Social work. A companion to learning*. London: Sage.

McCormack, B and Titchen, A (2006) Critical creativity: Melding, exploding, blending. *Education Action Research*, 14 (2), 239–66.

Mezirow, J (1991) *Transformative dimensions of adult learning*. San Francisco, CA: Jossey-Bass.

Oliver, M (1990) *The politics of disablement*. Basingstoke: Macmillan.

Ottewell, D and Marsden, C (2008) *Mystery man now has real name and family*. Report in *Oldham Advertiser*, free press, 11 September.

Pintrich, PR and DeGroot, EV (1990) Motivational and self-regulated learning components of classroom academic performance. *Journal of Educational Psychology*, 82 (1), 33–40. American Psychological Association: Washington DC.

Powell, JP and Andresen, LW (1985) Humour and teaching in higher education. *Studies in Higher Education*, 10 (1), 79–90. London: Routledge.

Rooney, K (ed.) (1999) *Encarta.* London: Bloomsbury.

Salovey, P and Mayer, JD (1990) Perceiving affective content in ambiguous visual stimuli: A component of emotional intelligence. *Journal of Personality Assessment*, 54, 772–81.

Salovey, P, Bedell, B, Detweiler, JB and Mayer, JD (1999) Coping intelligently: Emotional intelligence and the coping process, in CR Snyder (ed.) *Coping: The psychology of what works* (pp141–64). New York: Oxford University Press.

Schön, D (1986) *Educating the reflective practitioner*. Oxford: Jossey-Bass.

Taylor, C and White, S (2006) Knowledge and reasoning in social work: Educating for humane judgement. *British Journal of Social Work*, 36 (6), 937–54.

Thompson, A (1996) *Critical reasoning: A practical introduction*. London: Routledge.

Thompson, N (2006) *Anti-discriminatory practice*. BASW practical series. Bristol: Policy Press.

Thompson, S and Thompson, N (2008) *The critically reflective practitioner*. Basingstoke: Palgrave Macmillan.

Watkins, JM and Mohr, BJ (2001) *Appreciative Inquiry – Change at the speed of imagination*. San Fransisco, CA: Jossey-Bass/Pfeiffer.

Webb, SA (2006) *Social work in a risk society: Social and political perspectives*. Basingstoke: Palgrave.

Weber, L (1998) A conceptual framework for understanding race, class, gender and sexuality. *Psychology of Women Quarterly*, 22 (1), 13–32.

Wolters, C (1998) Self-regulated learning and college students' regulation of motivation. *Journal of Educational Psychology*, 90 (2), 224–35.

# Websites

www.criticalreading.com

www.kent.ac.uk/english/writingwebsite/writing/article3_p5.htm

www.mindtools.com

www.nationalcareforum.org.uk

http://news.bbc.co.uk/

www.noodletools.com/debbie/literacies/visual/diglitnews.pdf

www.questia.com

www.rottentomatoes.com

www.scie.org.uk

www.scie-socialcareonline.org.uk

www.skillsforcare.org.uk

http://writing.upenn.edu/critical/help_tips.html

# Index

Added to the page number 'f' denotes a figure, 'g' denotes the glossary and 't' denotes a table.